Salary Tutor

Salary Tutor

Learn the Salary Negotiation Secrets No One Ever Taught You

JIM HOPKINSON

BUSINESS PLUS

NEW YORK   BOSTON

Business Plus
Hachette Book Group
237 Park Avenue
New York, NY 10017
www.HachetteBookGroup.com

Business Plus is an imprint of Grand Central Publishing.
The Business Plus name and logo are trademarks of Hachette Book Group, Inc.

The publisher is not responsible for websites (or their content) that are not owned by the publisher.

Printed in the United States of America
First Edition: August 2011

10 9 8 7 6 5 4 3 2 1

Library of Congress Control Number: 2011922028

ISBN: 978-1-4555-0327-8

Contents

FROM THE AUTHOR
Why I Wrote This Book

Passion.

Millions of teachers, authors, parents, friends, clergy, poets, and musicians have tried to help others find their passions. But I'll tell you where you can find yours.

In your voice.

When you're speaking about something you're truly passionate about, there's a change in your tone. Your heart beats a little faster, your eyes get a little wider, and sometimes the thoughts and ideas cascade from your brain so quickly that they trip over themselves in a rush to exit your mouth.

Throughout my life, I've been passionate about many things, from cars and computers to sports and travel. But one constant passion has been career development. I love developing a mental picture of a person through their résumé, helping people go after their dream job, and guiding young professionals.

But while some might be ambivalent to the font on their cover letter or the benefits of networking, I've found the topic of salary negotiation ignites an equal amount of passion in every person I speak with.

I noticed that, without fail, people would light up at the mention of the topic and wanted to absorb as much information as humanly possible. The reason for this was that no one had ever sat them down and taught them the necessary skills. It was as if I were revealing a big secret.

I knew that sharing this information had enormous potential. Not only could people increase their income and standard of living, but also their happiness and self-esteem.

I decided to consolidate everything that I had learned into a single document. That document became a presentation that I gave as a class, and that class presentation evolved into this book.

Photo: Diana Levine (DianaLevine.com)

In my experience, people showed interest when I provided step-by-step instructions that could help them with negotiation. But it was when I wrapped the learning with personal, real-life examples, funny anecdotes, and narrative stories that they truly engaged with the content. Call it a "novel" approach, if you will.

They needed to learn the secrets of getting a higher salary, but wanted the experience to feel like a close personal friend was teaching them.

Thus, *Salary Tutor: Learn the Salary Negotiation Secrets No One Ever Taught You* was born.

Jim Hopkinson

CHAPTER 1

Introduction

Think back to your childhood.

What did you want to be when you grew up? Was it a firefighter, or a doctor, or an astronaut?

That's what you wanted when you were younger, but then life got in the way. When it came time to choose your college major, "space travel" was not among the choices. When you graduated, you were faced with college loans, everyday bills, and security deposits on your first apartment.

Suddenly your dream of being a firefighter or a doctor or an astronaut fades away, and you end up being a Junior Assistant Sales Representative, a Senior Manager of Customer Care, or an Associate Coordinator of Business Accounts.

However, those jobs are all fantastic, if you're passionate about what you do.

Yes, this is a book about salary negotiation. But before you worry about money, take the pillow test.

What's the pillow test?

1. When you go to bed, are you stressed about your job? Can you put your head down on the pillow at night and sleep peacefully?
2. When you wake up in the morning and take your head off the pillow, are you excited and eager to go to work?

What happens when you start and end your day with a good attitude about your career? Let me give you

Photo: NASA

a real-life example of this, which is called a "virtuous cycle." A virtuous cycle is a complex set of events that reinforces itself through a feedback loop. I like to tell the story of a "virtuous bicycle."

When I moved to Seattle, I made a lot of friends who shared with me their love of mountain biking. After a few rides with them, it became pretty clear that my existing bike was too outdated, too heavy, and not suited to the steep, rocky, slippery terrain of the Northwest.

A friend recommended that I buy an upgraded bike, one that cost well over a thousand dollars. In fact, he pulled out the glossy catalog, pointed to one, and said, "Now *this* would be the one you'd really love." I remember that it was $2,200. I had sticker shock. "Two grand? The one I have now was $499 when I bought it, and it was one of the more expensive models they offered. I could never spend more than $1,000."

Now, here was my fear. No matter which bike I chose, it was a huge amount of money for a new hobby.

What if it was more than what I needed? What if I decided to stop biking?

However, after weeks and weeks of research, I made a decision based on the best choice for me, which was the next model down from the one my friend recommended. I found an incredible deal, getting $600 off the full retail price of $1,800.

This is what happened. I was really excited about the bike, so I rode more. The more I rode, the more skilled I became. Since it was a better bike, I became a better rider. Because I became a better rider, I had more fun. The more fun I had, the more I wanted to ride. The more I rode, the more skilled I became. And the virtuous cycle just kept repeating.

You can look at it the same way with your job. If you start out by saying, "I love my job," then, generally, what's going to happen is you're going to get good at your job. If you're good at your job, you'll get a raise. When you get a raise, you'll like your job more. When you like your job more, you're probably going to do better at it. When you do better at your job, you will likely get noticed more. When you get noticed more, you'll get a promotion, and hopefully a pay increase as well.

If you follow your heart and do something you're passionate about, will you skip to work each morning

Jim on the bike

Photo: Jennifer Day

and be greeted with an unending flow of cash? No. But it's a good start, and it sure beats hating going to work every day for forty years. You still need to familiarize yourself with basic salary negotiation skills.

As the saying goes, "Do what you love, and the money will follow."

But, for everyone else, there's Salary Tutor.

Notice to panicked job seekers

I realize that many of you might have picked up this book days or even hours before an interview. The thought races through your mind: *Oh my gosh, they're probably going to ask me about salary in this interview, and I have no idea what to say. I better find out quickly.*

If that's the case, feel free to jump ahead to chapter 6 to get a crash course on the step-by-step fundamentals.

However, I urge you to return and pick up from the beginning to get a fuller understanding of the entire process. For those with a little more time, sit back and enjoy the story.

2 CHAPTER
Passion and Research

Okay, you've made an important first step. As you'll see from some stats later on, the most important step in the entire negotiation process isn't what you say or when you say it, it's simply deciding to negotiate in the first place…to decide that you're going to arm yourself with information and ask for what you deserve.

There are two reasons you are in good hands with me:

1. I've been able to turn things I'm passionate about into a career.
2. I love doing ridiculous amounts of research around a topic.

So who am I and what am I passionate about?

1. I'm passionate about sports. I'm a huge sports fan, and I was able to turn that into a career at ESPN.com, the number one sports website on the Internet. I spent seven years in their fantasy sports group, and fantasy sports is all about research.

2. I'm passionate about technology. What kind of career have I been able to turn it into? First, I worked for a software company. Next, I worked for a tech start-up. Last, I landed a job at Wired.com, the online home of *Wired* magazine, the award-winning publication that covers the ever-changing world of innovation and how it affects technology, business, science, and pop culture. I am constantly and obsessively researching the latest technology, preparing detailed, analytical reports for my job. I also do deep-dive research into marketing and pop culture trends for my blog and podcast, *The Hopkinson Report*.

3. Last, I am passionate about career development and teaching others. I've taught classes at NYU, cofounded an entrepreneurial meetup group in Manhattan, guest-lectured at universities, written articles about job search tips, and presented at large companies such as General

Electric. I excitedly help others with their résumés and cover letters, role-play interviewing skills with friends, and have served as a mentor for a dozen young professionals. At *Wired*, my renowned internship program is as competitive as it is rewarding.

Here is what I found in my work experience:

When it comes to salary negotiation, no one teaches you this stuff.

They don't teach it to you in high school, they don't teach it to you in college, and there are few, if any, classes on salary negotiation. My friends never bring it up in conversation, and it's not something that my parents taught me. Even in college I don't recall career services covering the topic with graduates about to enter the workforce.

The human resources department at your own job certainly isn't going to tell you ways to get extra money. And even if you look at leading job search sites, they might have a few articles about it, but none of them go into enough depth in a single blog post to give you any truly valuable information.

I wondered, is it just me?

So I went over to Google.
I searched for "interview tips," and more than 50 million results came up.
Then I searched for "resume tips," and almost 40 million results came up.
Then I searched for "salary negotiation tips," and 508,000 results came up.

Then I went over to Amazon.com to look for books on the subject.
I searched for the keyword "interview" and found more than 40,000 books.
Then I searched for "resume" and saw nearly 5,000 books.
But for "salary negotiation," there were just 139 books on this important subject.

So I read.
And I researched.
And I talked to people.
And I practiced.
And I came up with a plan to share with you.

Google Search Results

Image: Jim Hopkinson / Erin Fitzsimmons

First, let me answer some questions:

Can I *guarantee* you success? No.
Is it *easy* to get a raise when the economy is bad? No.
Will this work for *all* positions in *all* companies? No.
Will it work equally well for *current* jobs versus *new* jobs? No.
Will it work equally well for both *young* and *experienced* job seekers? No.

So what will *this book do for you?*

Regardless of outcome, I believe that I can help you come out of your next interview with the ability to answer two key questions:

1. Was I prepared?
2. Did I do everything I could?

Those are your two goals. By the end of this book, you'll be armed with all the information you need to achieve this level of confidence.

CHAPTER 3
Salary vs. Job Satisfaction

Let's look at a case study of Kevin from London (not his real name). He applied for a finance job in New York City and received a very reasonable offer. He was very, very excited about the move to the United States and this awesome new opportunity. That night he went out with some friends to a local pub, and he asked his mates for advice as he told them the exciting news.

He asked several questions about the big move, including, "What do you think—should I try and negotiate on the salary?" His friends told him, "No way, don't blow it. Just be happy you got the job. You don't want to risk losing it." So he accepted the initial offer.

1. *Was he prepared?*
   No, he wasn't familiar with the negotiation process.

2. *Did he do everything he could?*
   No, he didn't make a counteroffer.

Fast-forward a few weeks and he starts his new job in New York. He's still very excited, and he makes a new friend at orientation. They have the same background, they start the same day, and they have the exact same title. That Friday night after work, they decide to go for drinks to celebrate their first week on the job. They have a few beers, discuss the people in the office, and the conversation eventually turns to salary. As the fifth and last Guinness is tipped back, the clock strikes midnight, and it comes out…that the other guy makes…

Photos: Jim Hopkinson

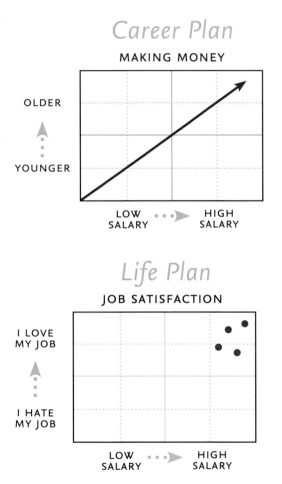

Career Plan

MAKING MONEY

OLDER

YOUNGER

LOW SALARY ••• ► HIGH SALARY

Life Plan

JOB SATISFACTION

I LOVE MY JOB

I HATE MY JOB

LOW SALARY ••• ► HIGH SALARY

Image: Jim Hopkinson/Erin Fitzsimmons

. . . $20,000 more than Kevin.

To put it mildly, that put a major damper on Kevin's excitement. You may think, *Oh, he can just work hard and get raises and catch up.* But you know what? That other person is going to get raises at a similar rate. So, the other person who started with $20,000 more will almost always be ahead of Kevin in terms of salary.

So now you may be asking, "Well, Mr. Smarty Pants, how much do you make now?" Well, am I going to tell you my current salary? No. But will I tell you how I got here? Yes, I will.

A lot of people have a misconception that a graph of your career plan simply goes from the bottom left to the top right and says "the older I get, the higher my salary"—and that's not always true.

The way I look at it, yours should be a life plan based not on making money but on job satisfaction. So, on the Y axis on the left, it goes from "I hate my job" on the bottom to "I love my job" at the top. And on the X axis, it goes from "low salary" on the left to "high salary" on the right.

Look at this grid and think about how happy you are, how satisfied you are with your job.

Are you in the bottom left quadrant, where you have "I hate my job and I have a low salary"? Well, that's a position that you definitely don't want to be in, and hopefully that's why you're reading this and looking for a new job and/or more money.

In the bottom right you have "I hate my job, but have a high salary." Perhaps you are a lawyer or an investment banker, someone who gets paid very, very well but has a brutal work schedule that doesn't allow for a balanced and fulfilling life.

People in the upper left quadrant have low salaries but love their jobs. Maybe they're just starting out, or they're schoolteachers, or artists.

And, of course, what you are aiming to get to is in the upper right quadrant. Who does not want to love their job *and* have a high salary?

Also, remember that a high salary doesn't have to be millions of dollars or even six figures. Studies have shown that once basic needs are met—that is, when you can afford to pay for your shelter, your clothes, and feed your family comfortably—major increases in salary do not equate to major increases in happiness.

So, when looking at my salary history, do you think it will be a straight forty-five-degree angle from the lower left to the top right? Let's find out.

Before we delve into that, let's take a moment to look at **Tutor Test 1.**

$Tutor
Test 1

Sit back, do an honest assessment, and really think about your current work situation. Then ask yourself the following questions.

What is your happiness level on a scale of 1 to 10?

1   2   3   4   5   6   7   8   9   10

◄ ● ►

Are you doing something you're passionate about?

_____

_____

_____

Do you feel that you're being paid a fair salary for your value?

_____

_____

_____

CHAPTER 4

Jim's Salary History
Case Study and Lessons Learned

Okay, let's talk about my salary history. When I was in college, I was consumed with things like classes, homework, parties, my fraternity, and intramural sports. I was pretty much immune (naïve?) to outside forces for four years, and I really wasn't looking at the external job market.

As I approached graduation in my last semester, I started spending a lot more time in our career services center, thinking about my future. I remember there was some kind of chart that listed the average starting salary for every major at the school. I dragged my finger past Accounting and Actuarial and Communications until I arrived at my major, Computer Information Systems. I glanced to the right, and the number was very specific, something like...

$$\$41,423$$

And with that, I was really excited that I was going to graduate in a few months, and I was going to make $41,423. After all, that was what the chart said.

Well, what was the reality?

After graduating in May 1991, the unemployment rate during the following nine months while I was job searching peaked at 8.2 percent. To put that into perspective, that was the highest rate of unemployment the United States would see for the next eighteen years.

It would take a crash in our real estate market, the collapse of major banking institutions, and 5 million jobs lost to eclipse that mark, as unemployment reached 8.5 percent in January 2009 and 10.6 percent in January 2010. So if you think you had it pretty bad during that time frame, I assure you that things weren't so rosy when I walked across the stage and accepted my diploma.

Unemployment rate
The percent of the labor force that is unemployed, not seasonally adjusted.

Data source: U.S. Bureau of Labor Statistics - Last updated January 12, 2011

Image: Google Public Data using U.S. Bureau of Labor Statistics

To keep track of things: What was my starting salary upon graduation? It was $0.00.

Since my newly minted résumé wasn't breaking through the thousands of more qualified people looking for work and I could not get a job, I decided to do an internship. I was making zero money at the internship, but I was gaining a little bit of experience.

So now I was in the internship, my salary still at $0.00.

Actually, it wasn't quite that high, because during my daily commute from the suburbs of Boston into Cambridge on the Southeast Expressway, my car—a 1975 Dodge Dart—blew its transmission. I needed a way to get around, so I had no choice but to repair my car, digging into what little savings I had to do so.

If you're keeping score, my annual salary so far in the year I graduated college was *negative* $1,000.

Finally, by the end of 1991, I had used up much of my savings and I had to have *some* kind of income. I stopped doing the internship and I got a job at Staples. Yes, Staples, the Office Superstore.

I filled out an application to the best of my abilities, dropped it off with the manager on duty, and went home. By that point, I had been rejected by dozens and dozens of companies, so I was shocked when I walked in the door of my parents' house and the phone was ringing. Sure enough, it was Staples, calling to offer me a job. It was only a ten-minute ride home; that was how long it took them to see my résumé and want to hire me.

In retrospect, *of course* they did. Even though I was a little beat down and used to getting rejected by larger companies, how often was it that Staples got an application from an honors graduate in CIS wanting to work in the computer and copier department of their retail store? They hired me immediately.

How much was I making? I believe it was $6 an hour, so let's say my annual salary would have been around $9,000 a year. Needless to say, there was no negotiation to be had at this position.

After a few months at Staples, in the beginning of 1992, I started to see a lot more help-wanted ads in the paper, and the economy seemed to be picking up. I said to myself, "Yes! The economy is recovering and I'm going to finally land a job and start making $41,423!"

Jim poses with his Dodge Dart.

Photo: Jim Hopkinson

$9,000

$0
SALARY UPON
GRADUATION

$0
INTERNSHIP

-$1,000
CAR BLOWS
TRANSMISSION

HOURLY RETAIL
AT STAPLES

Ironically, it was this part-time job at Staples that directly led me to my first real job as a Technical Support Representative. I was hired by a company called Spinnaker Software, and it made programs that were similar to today's Microsoft Office. These programs also happened to be preinstalled on nearly every computer we sold at Staples. So when I got the interview and the first question was "So, Jim, what do you do right now?" I was able to answer honestly, "Well, I sell *your* software."

The interview process went really well, and I was told that HR would be calling to offer me a job. Finally! I'm going to get that $41,423. When I got to the negotiation point, the HR person told me all the details, and then said, "The starting salary is $20,000."

Ouch. It was at this point that I probably came up with the term *the Evil HR Lady*.

Finally, my first chance at negotiation. I launched into all the bullet points that I had written down, saying that I had real-world experience with their products, how I graduated with honors, and how I felt that I deserved something higher in the range. The mean HR woman quickly replied, "Everyone starts at $20,000. Do you want the job or not?"

So, according to my rules, was I prepared? Yes.

I had written down all the things that I wanted to say during the negotiation, highlighting my strengths as a candidate.

Did I do everything I could? Yes.

Although I didn't receive more money because the salary was fixed for every person at this entry-level position, at least I had made a counteroffer, and I knew that everyone at the same level as me was starting on an even playing field.

I was there six months and I got a raise to $22,000. After another six months, I got a raise to $24,000. And in just another six months, I got a raise to $26,000. Things were going great.

Introducing the
Evil HR Lady

© *iStockphoto.com/vitalijlang*

$20,000

ENTRY-LEVEL AT
SPINNAKER

14

$22,000

RAISE!

$24,000

RAISE!

$26,000

RAISE!

$0

LAYOFF

And then just like that, there was an announcement about some kind of merger, they told us that all technical support would be moved to Atlanta, and the entire department got laid off.

My annual salary was back to $0.00.

However, during those eighteen months, the economy had continued to improve. Spinnaker allowed us to stay on the job for a few weeks while we job-searched and went on interviews. At least one person in the office per day showed up in a suit, then came back from their interview saying, "I just got a job offer for $30,000!…I just got a job offer for $35,000!" So finally, I was ready to start making some real money.

Then one day my supervisor came to me (and only me, if I took him at his word) and said, "I have a friend who works at a start-up, and he's looking to take on someone new. He asked me for a recommendation, and you were the only person I knew I could recommend."

I said, "Wow, what's a start-up? Is that something like Yahoo! or Google, where I'm going to make $35,000 *plus* get millions of dollars in potential stock options?"

Well, there's actually no way I could have said that.

Why? Remember that this was 1993, and Yahoo! and Google hadn't even been *founded* yet. So, I guess the comparison at the time would be Microsoft.

However, it wasn't one of *those* start-ups.

This was a company just getting off the ground, keeping costs cut to the bone, and getting by however they could. Nevertheless, I was excited. This was something completely new, and I hit it off immediately with the VP of Development.

I liked the idea of building something, I liked the people I met, and I was fired up to get started. All that was left was the compensation, and as I held my breath, my future boss came to me and said, "The starting salary is $26,000."

Yes, the *exact* same amount that I was making at my current position, and nowhere near $41,423. I was devastated.

I really wanted to take this new job; I really wanted to take a chance at this start-up. So I called my future boss one night, and although it could be considered a salary negotiation, it really was just a conversation that came from brutal honesty on my part.

NASDAQ: YHOO

Yahoo: 1997–2000

Image: Jim Hopkinson/Erin Fitzsimmons

$26,000

OFFER!

Nervously I began, "Bill, here's the situation. I really want to take the job, I'm really excited about what you're doing, and I really want to work there."

He said, "What's the problem?"

I said, "You offered me $26,000, and that's the exact same amount that I was making at my current job. I know you guys are trying to keep costs low, and I know that you told me that you'd be able to take care of me when the company started doing well, but I just feel—"

At that moment he abruptly cut me off midsentence and asked, "How much do you need?"

Wow. This caught me completely by surprise. Numbers started racing through my head, I stalled for a second by saying, "Ummm," then I just kind of blurted out, "$28,000?"

Again, he abruptly said, "Let me get right back to you."

No more than ten minutes later, the phone rang and he said, "Yup, we can do $28,000. When can you start?"

So, let's recap.

Was I prepared? Somewhat.

I knew to ask for more money, but I didn't know exactly what to say.

Did I do everything I could? Somewhat.

I did counteroffer, and I did get an 8 percent raise, but it definitely could have been more if I had been more prepared. Would he have given me $29,000? $30,000? I'm pretty sure he would have.

Here's the good news:

Because I took a chance in life, and I took a risk and went to this start-up, when they started doing well, they had a lot more flexibility to reward good performance. My friends who took the safer job for $30,000 got that initial raise, but were then getting a 2, 3, or 5 percent cost-of-living increase every year.

On the flip side, what happened with me was that I got a 14 percent raise to $32,000 at my first annual review. The next year I got a 13 percent raise to $36,000.

$28,000

NEGOTIATED
8% RAISE IN
STARTING SALARY

$32,000

14% RAISE

$36,000

13% RAISE

The next year I got a 17 percent raise to $42,000.

And the year after that another 14 percent raise, to $48,000.

So, I was quickly able to go from $28,000 to $48,000 within a few short years.

By 1998 I had been there four years and had learned just about everything I was going to learn there. The company was making CD-ROM-based training programs, and I thought this new "Internet" thing seemed kind of cool.

I went on a run on New Year's Day, 1998, and vowed that by the time my apartment lease was up at the end of August, I would accomplish the following:

- Move to another part of the country.
- Get a job in the Internet industry.
- Work in a career that I was insanely passionate about.

Fast-forward eight months. The tale of how, on August 31, 1998, I started my first day at my dream job in sports at ESPN.com, three thousand miles away in Seattle, is a whole other story for a different book.

The bottom line was, I had detailed my specific goals, made it happen, aced the interviews, and landed my dream job. I was currently making $48,000, and ESPN told me they were going to make an offer. I said to myself, *Oh boy, this is awesome. Amazing. Perfect. I can't believe everything has fallen into place. They're probably going to offer me $60,000, $70,000, or even $80,000 per year.*

Once again I had laid out my bullet points and was eagerly awaiting the call from HR in Seattle. I sneaked into a private conference room at my office to take the call, during which they listed out the benefits, and then made me an offer of…

…$40,000—a 17 percent pay cut from what I had been making. Ouch again.

$42,000

$48,000

17% RAISE

14% RAISE

$40,000

ESPN's
OFFER

17

Undeterred, I went through my bullet points, regurgitated my rehearsed script, reiterated my skill set, and told them my industry research showed people in that position were making more.

The Evil HR Lady countered by saying that Disney (which owned ESPN) had just completed their *own* survey, comparing their compensation with everyone else's in the industry and readjusting where needed, and that this was in line with *their* numbers. Touché.

So I had another dilemma. Do I take this dream job? Do I take this pay cut?

The answer, of course, which took about a millisecond, was *absolutely*. This was a chance of a lifetime to work in sports, enter an emerging industry, explore a new city, and do something I was truly passionate about.

So once again, let's look at what happened here:

Was I prepared? Yes.

I did research what the market was paying, made a strong counteroffer, and made my case why I should get more.

Did I do everything I could? Yes again.

I tried very hard to get a raise. I used some techniques and it turned out the salary was locked for that position. So, I felt that I had at least done the research, made a counteroffer, and done everything I could.

I also want to bring up an important point: It's not always about the salary.

1. The job was in Seattle, Washington, a state that does not collect income tax. This saved me thousands, not to mention ESPN was picking up all moving costs.

2. ESPN had great health-care benefits, which were less expensive than at my current company.

3. They offered a free, unlimited gym membership at one of the best athletic clubs in Seattle (worth $500–$1,000 a year), and also threw in a free Costco membership (another $50 a year). These were actually perks that I would use, saving me more out-of-pocket expenses.

4. Their corporate travel group had a deal where employees would receive about 50 percent off all United Airlines flights. Considering I would be flying from Seattle to see my family in Boston several times per year, that would be an enormous cost savings.

I calculated that even though I was receiving a salary of only $40,000, the actual worth was easily $45,000 or more.

Jim's dream job included a trip to the Super Bowl.

Photo: Jim Hopkinson

Last, c'mon. This was a dream job. They were paying me to talk about fantasy football for a living! I should have been paying *them* $40,000 a year.

And because I was doing something I loved, I excelled in the job, got promoted quickly, and by the time I had my first review, they bumped me back up to around $48,000. That means that even though I had to take a pay cut to invest in my dream job, I made back the ROI (return on investment) within a year.

By 1999, the environment in my given industry was the polar opposite of when I started my career. The early '90s in Boston saw the downfall of large computer firms such as Digital Equipment Corporation, which went from having a "no layoffs" policy to letting go six thousand people in 1991 and losing $300 million in the first quarter of 1992.

I still remember walking into the start-up each morning and finding piles of DEC résumés lying next to the fax machine, from dozens of laid-off, middle-aged computer gurus with years and years of experience applying for the entry-level jobs we had posted.

By contrast, the Internet boom gripped Seattle like a fever, as companies scrambled to hire and retain the best employees as hopes, stock options, market caps, and net worth soared (at least on paper).

I knew things were out of control the day my boss called me into his office to tell me they were giving me something called a "retention bonus."

During the boom, scores of people were leaving their jobs to go to the latest, greatest start-up. It seemed there was at least one "farewell" e-mail per day from someone jumping ship for the next great dotcom. So many companies in our industry were fighting for these talented employees that ESPN actually paid me a fairly large amount of money to simply *do nothing except stay at my dream job*. Sounded pretty good to me.

For the next eight years, I received title upgrades and salary bumps, eventually transferring to the New York City office and finally to ESPN's new mobile division.

Looking back at the scorecard:

Was I prepared? Yes.

Each time I got a review, I had diligently documented all the accomplishments that I achieved in the past year.

Did I do everything I could? Somewhat.

While I supported my accomplishments with relevant data and made sure I was being recognized at each of my standard annual reviews, I never went out of my way to ask for a larger promotion or raise. Because I failed to step back and look at the big picture, there was a certain period where my career stagnated when I should have been more aggressive.

But there I was, still doing a job that thousands of people would love to have. Everything was perfect, right?

That is, until October 2006, when they closed the mobile division I was working in and I got laid off again. Head over to the lifetime salary grid and bring that back down to $0.00 per year.

But at this point, I felt that I had a much better grasp of my career goals. I was in my thirties, had fifteen years of experience, had built a strong network, and had wisely put some money aside in case a situation like this arose. For many people, especially those with a family to support, a layoff can be devastating. Fortunately, I had seen this coming and prepared for it, and thus had a little time to reflect. In doing so, I took a much-needed vacation to South Africa to think about my next plan.

To quickly sum up the last few years of my career: When I got back from vacation I was laser-focused, and I started targeting only specific industries, companies, and jobs that I was passionate about. During this break I also did incredible amounts of research and practiced interviewing and negotiation, so that by the time I had my interview at *Wired*, I could say:

Was I prepared? Good Lord, yes.

Did I do everything I could? Absolutely 100 percent.

I will later teach you the techniques that will allow you to answer those questions the same way.

As you can see, it's not simply a straight line from your starting salary all the way up to a huge salary as your career progresses. Far from it. There can be lots of highs and lows, multiple layoffs, several bumps, and taking a step back in order to take two steps forward.

Looking back on that graph, I think I did pretty well, but I wondered how much more I could have earned if I had proactively asked for raises and title changes on a consistent basis, and negotiated salary in a tactical manner whenever I had the opportunity.

So I did the math.

Of the four major jobs I'd had:

The good

- Asked for more money at every offer
- Pursued a career based on my passions
- Took risks and targeted growth industries
- Was given raises based on hard work

The bad

- Could have been more proactive at certain stages
- Stagnated at certain parts of my career and stayed in certain positions for too long

Result

- Approximately 12 percent average annual raises

Let's see how those numbers shape up against the rest of the workforce.

Jim's salary history shows steady growth, as well as a few decreases.

Image: Jim Hopkinson/Erin Fitzsimmons

5 CHAPTER
By the Numbers
What the Average Raise Is, and What You Should Do about It

After calculating the annual raises that I had received throughout my career, I wondered how that compared with the national averages.

- *Money* magazine projected the average pay raise to be 3.3 percent in 2009 and 5.6 percent for top performers, while a World at Work survey projected similar results (3.6 and 5.2 percent, respectively).

- Employers surveyed by consulting and services company Mercer said that the average pay increase was expected to be 2.8 percent in 2011, up from 2.7 percent in 2010.

- The average federal worker's pay raise was 3.8 percent in 2008, 3.9 percent in 2009, and 2 percent in 2010.

What this tells me is that, though the numbers may change from year to year (depending on the economy, the industry you work in, and where you get your data), the increases were never going to be dramatic. Clearly I had done fairly well seizing opportunities, averaging two to six times the national average. But you don't need to hit double-digit raises to have things pay off in the big picture. When it comes to negotiating salary, every single dollar counts.

You might ask yourself, *Can a measly 1 percent increase in salary really make a difference?*

Well, let's do the math to graph the career path I just took you through. If you start out at age twenty-one and retire at age sixty-five, and you start your annual income at $20,000 and get 5 percent raises, you would accrue lifetime earnings of $3 million. • • • • • • • • • • →

However, even if you negotiate just a teeny-tiny bit and get 6 percent raises instead of 5 percent raises, your lifetime earnings jump to $4 million. So just a 1 percent increase in earnings will equal an additional $1 million in salary over your lifetime.

If you were nervous about asking for that extra 1 percent, just think about having an extra seven figures in earnings in your lifetime. And if you can make some key career choices and average 12 percent or more, you really set yourself up for a more comfortable lifestyle. It's something that every person in the workplace should have in the back of their mind come negotiation time.

Why is this even more important for women?

According to the Bureau of Labor Statistics:

- More women are in the workforce.
  - Women made up 60 percent of the workforce in the 2000s, up from 43 percent in 1970.
- More women are better educated.
  - Women age 25–64 in the labor force with a college degree tripled from 1970 (11 percent) to 2008 (36 percent).
- Women are contributing more, but still far less than men.
  - Working wives contributed only 36 percent of their families' incomes in 2007, up from 27 percent in 1970.

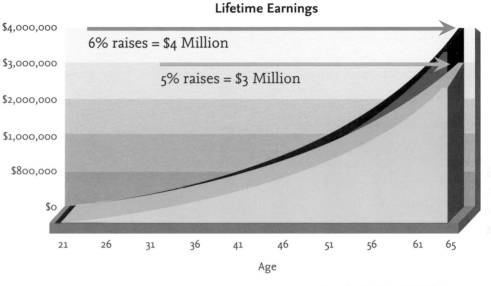

Lifetime Earnings

6% raises = $4 Million

5% raises = $3 Million

$4,000,000
$3,000,000
$2,000,000
$1,000,000
$800,000
$0

Age: 21 26 31 36 41 46 51 56 61 65

Image: Jim Hopkinson/Erin Fitzsimmons

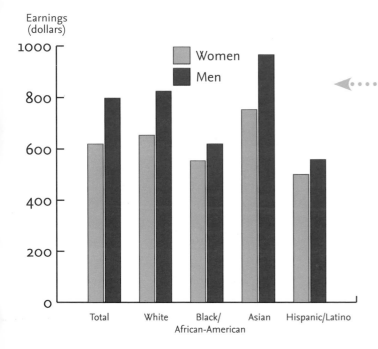

Earnings (dollars)

Women
Men

1000
800
600
400
200
0

Total · White · Black/African-American · Asian · Hispanic/Latino

Median weekly earnings of full-time wage and salary workers, by sex, race, and Hispanic or Latino ethnicity, 2008 annual wages

Image: U.S. Bureau of Labor Statistics/Erin Fitzsimmons

- More women are self-employed.
  - In 2008, 38 percent of women were self-employed, up from 27 percent in 1976.

Among full-time wage and salary earners in 2008, women earned 80 cents for every $1 that men earned. While this is up significantly from 62 cents in 1979, it is still 20 percent less. This breakdown also holds true, with variations, depending on race.

Does the topic of negotiating salary make you nervous?

If so, you are not alone.

A survey of five hundred women done by negotiatingwomen.com revealed that 20 percent—one in five!—*never* negotiate their salaries. Clearly you can't gain the maximum amount of income that you deserve if you're not even in the game.

Remember our goals. You want to be able to say:

1. *I was prepared.*

2. *I did everything I could.*

Are most women prepared?

Not all of them—19 percent said they were *not prepared at all* for surprises that might come up during a negotiation.

Can most women say they did everything they could (such as counteroffer)?

No, 16 percent of women say they *never* counteroffer.

Historically, women have been much worse at negotiation (but men can learn from this, too). In their book *Women Don't Ask*, authors Linda Babcock and Sara Laschever talk about the following scenario, which I'll call:

The authors did a study in which they asked students to play the word game Boggle. They were told beforehand that they would be paid between $3 and $10. Each student played four games, and then was told, "Here's $3. Is that okay?"

If students just *complained* (and many did), the leader of the study did nothing. However, if students *asked* for $10, they were given $10. What were the results?

Nine times as many men as women asked for more money!

The authors tried to find reasons why this happened, but all students ranked their ability at performing the test equally (so they didn't feel they should have less pay for subpar work), and both men and women complained at an equal rate. It was simply that for men, unhappiness meant they did something about it.

Now many of you might say:

- "I hate negotiation."
- "I try to avoid conflict."
- "I figure they know what they are willing to pay."
- "I just get so nervous and don't know what to say."

And I won't lie to you:

- You'll need to do some homework.
- You'll need to do some practice.
- The time you spend across from your future boss or the HR manager may be the most uncomfortable few minutes of your life.

But...

- if you get excited about this,
- if you are prepared,

Photo: Public Domain via Wikipedia

- if you do everything you can,
- if you can be strong and not cave for just those few minutes,
- and you nail this…

The results could include…

- higher salary and benefits,
- increased lifetime earnings,
- respect from your employer, and
- clear focus and (renewed) excitement in your new or current position.

From personal experience, when I lined up my interview at *Wired* for the job I truly wanted:

- I spent *a week* researching and preparing for a one-hour first interview.
- When that went well, I prepared even more. In fact, I practiced and role-played salary negotiation for my second interview for *eight straight hours*.

Why would I spend so much time? Three reasons:

1. Remember that I was unemployed at the time…errr, contemplating my next move and brainstorming career options from the top of Table Mountain in Cape Town half a world away. It was a lot easier to devote everything I had to this since I did not have a full-time job—but even if I did, I would have spent considerable time preparing.

2. What else have *you* spent eight hours doing? Rehearsing the two or three key phrases to be used during my negotiation for hours on end may seem like a lot of time, but think about how quickly eight hours goes by in your life on less mundane tasks. Have you spent that long researching a vacation, watching YouTube videos, uploading photos to Facebook, or viewing season-long series such as *Lost*, *American Idol*, or *The Bachelor*? The math is pretty simple… if you ever watched a season of the show *24*, that's three times the amount.

3. The stakes were at their highest. Why the laser focus? I knew that there were very few targeted companies that I wanted to work for and this was one of them. For any given job, hundreds of people apply, but very few get interviews. This was my chance and I knew it.

Photo: Robert Shanes

Once I sensed they were interested and asked me about salary, the balance of power shifts from me trying to *get* the job to them *making sure they got me*. That moment is when I have the most leverage. During that five-minute conversation, I knew the things I said and the way I said them could make me thousands, and that future increases in salary were not guaranteed or might be a year or more away.

I also wanted to make sure I armed myself with as much knowledge as possible to even the playing field against the person I was sitting across from. Consider this: The Evil HR Lady you're dealing with may negotiate salaries with candidates several times *per week*. For those who tend to stay in jobs for the long term, you may do this only a few times in *your life*, which puts you at a distinct disadvantage when the two of you square off.

However, stats from the Bureau of Labor Statistics have shown that as much as 40 percent of the workforce changes jobs in a year. That means thousands of people are being asked about salary every day. The BLS also released a report in September 2010 that examined the number of jobs held by people born between 1957 and 1964. The findings showed these Baby Boomers held an average of eleven jobs in their career.

When I read that number, I was actually shocked that it was that high. After all, isn't the older generation supposed to value company loyalty and longtime employment? Isn't "job hopping" seen as a negative thing? As someone firmly entrenched in Generation X, my career would indicate so, with only four jobs in nineteen years. My father's early career was similar, as he held only two jobs from 1973 to 1993.

And trumping both of us, during college I did an internship at the Bank of Boston, where my supervisor retired the second summer I worked there. I seem to remember that he took advantage of a bank policy that allowed him to retire not because he had reached the age of sixty-five, but because of an alternative option based on years of service. How many years? Forty-four! That's right: he'd had the same employer from age eighteen to sixty-two.

© iStockphoto.com/vitalijlang

That is clearly not the case today. In a 2010 *New York Times* article called "What Is It About 20-Somethings?" Robin Marantz Henig notes that young adults in Generation Y—also known as Echo Boomers—will go through an average of seven jobs in their twenties alone.

Thus in a typical forty-four-year career, they might find themselves with ten, fifteen, or even twenty jobs, with each change an opportunity to negotiate.

Tutor
Test 2

Think about previous negotiations, and jot down answers to these questions:

What kind of preparation did you do?

_____

_____

_____

How many hours did you spend preparing?

_____

_____

_____

How much money did you leave on the table?

_____

_____

_____

The goal is to avoid mistakes of the past.

CHAPTER 6

Defeating the Evil HR Lady

10 Steps to Effectively Negotiate Your Salary

You're up against the Evil HR Lady. Let's learn how to defeat her!

KEY STEPS TO SUCCESS

Step 1: Do your homework

Step 2: Network, network, network

Step 3: Preparing your "IRS document"

Step 4: Don't get eliminated

Step 5: Navigating the first interview

Step 6: The no-win question

Step 7: The "Right Back at Ya" Method

Step 8: 30 seconds to glory

Step 9: According to my research

Step 10: Take 'em for all they're worth

© iStockphoto.com/vitalijlang

Ready?

Let's do it.

Step 1: Do your homework

The first step in negotiating does not take place at the negotiation table but at the computer and out in the field. You must thoroughly research and find out what the salary range is for the job you are seeking for someone with your skills. This is a very important first step, because you will need this data during the negotiation.

How do you find that out? The easy ways are:

- It is stated in the job advertisement.
- The person who told you about the job knows the salary range.
- The job has a fixed salary for all candidates.

But it's not always that easy.

Furthermore, discussing salary can be a taboo subject.

There was an old TV commercial for IBM's web security and their "ebusiness solutions," showing two hackers sitting at computers in the dark. The guy is frantically tapping away at the keyboard, before exclaiming that he has broken into the personnel database, where he can see a list of salaries. His female cohort examines the list, and points out that one senior VP earns about *half* what another one earns. Then she adds, "I bet he doesn't know that." The other hacker pauses, flashes an evil grin, and taps at the keyboard again. He then kicks back and replies, "Sure he does. I just e-mailed everybody in the company."

Am I encouraging you to hack into company files to access this information? No. It's not always easy to find out what a salary is for a given position, but you need to get close. And actually, there are more ways than you think to find out what the ballpark number is.

Think of it as getting an estimate to have someone put a new roof on your house. You want a variety of different sources. Let's say your brother-in-law says he can replace the roof and tells you it will be about $3,000. Hmmm. Is that a good price? Or not?

Then you're at Home Depot and ask the guy there how much it would be to repair a roof, and he says he figures about $10,000. Now wait a minute—that's a huge difference. How can you tell who is right? Well, you keep going.

You start searching on Google, and you see quotes of $5,000 and $7,000. Then you get a contractor to come over to give you an estimate, and he quotes you $5,500. Then you're talking to your cousin a week later about the bad weather, and he says the roof of his small house was leaking and he paid $4,000 to repair it. Last, you reach out to an old friend on Facebook because you know he used to work in construction, and he guesses around $6,000 since he knows how big your house is.

So, does this mean you'll know *exactly* how much it will cost when it comes down to negotiating with the contractor? No. But you've done your homework and now know that your original range of $3,000 to $10,000 can be narrowed down to the $5,000–$7,000 range with a certain degree of confidence.

Now take those numbers, add an extra zero, and pretend it's a job you're going for.

Someone might tell you a starting salary might be $30,000, and some might say as high as $100,000. But as you do your analysis, use social media, tap into more sources, reflect on what you are making now, and note what skills you bring to the table, you could deduce that the job is in the $50,000–$70,000 range.

starting salary data|

Search

I recommend taking a dual approach: *online research* and *personal networking*.

Advantages of online research

> You can discover a lot of data in a short amount of time.
>
> You can check numbers from all over the country.
>
> Many sites have filters to customize your skills for a particular position.
>
> It can reflect up-to-the-minute market conditions.

Disadvantages of online research

> You may not be able to target your specific job or industry.
>
> People might lie online and overinflate their salaries.
>
> Some data may be old and not reflect market conditions.

Advantages of personal networking

> You can target contacts that work for the specific company you're interviewing with.
>
> A good source will know exactly what the job pays now.
>
> You'll get better results if the job is highly specialized or unique to your area.

Disadvantages of personal networking

> It can be difficult to track down the exact people you need to speak with.
>
> A smaller pool of sources might skew data.

Here are three valuable sources for online research, with a few examples of popular websites in each category.

Type 1: Job sites

> Monster.com/HotJobs.com
>
> CareerBuilder.com
>
> Craigslist.org
>
> TheLadders.com

HOW TO USE THEM

If the job you're going for doesn't list a salary, filter through hundreds of similar jobs and find ones that *do* post salary ranges.

Type 2: Salary information sites

PayScale.com

Salary.com

Glassdoor.com

HOW TO USE THEM

Sites like PayScale.com and Salary.com allow you to enter all your relevant information to see how you compare with others.

Glassdoor.com is a great resource. How does it work? If you enter your company name, title, salary, and other information anonymously, it lets you review their database of salaries that other people like you have contributed. It also lets you write reviews for companies.

Want to know what it's like to work at Microsoft and how much it pays?

At the beginning of 2011 they had:

- More than 12,000 salaries listed for more than 700 jobs
- 1,800 reviews on what it's like to work there
- 575 entries on the interviewing process
- 3,700 job openings

Clearly, you can gain some great insight.

Type 3: Social media

Facebook

Twitter

LinkedIn

HOW TO USE THEM

With Facebook and Twitter, you can detail your job search efforts and reach out to people in your network. Make sure not to simply ask people for jobs, but build a relationship with them and ask for advice.

With LinkedIn, I recommend a two-pronged approach:

1. Page through your network and the network of friends to target people who are working at jobs that seem interesting. For example, if you want to work in the medical field, search for contacts who are working at hospitals and companies that interest you.

2. Do research on your own for places you want to work, and then find a connection. For example, if you have an interview coming up at Massachusetts General Hospital, search through contacts in the Boston area and find someone who also works there.

Step 2: Network, network, network

Every job searcher should know that studies say upward of 80 percent of jobs are found through *networking.*

Let me repeat that: *Nearly 80 percent of jobs are found through networking.*

That means that if you are still job-searching, the vast majority of your time should be spent reaching out to people, going on informational interviews, asking people out to coffee or lunch, attending industry meetings, and joining groups in your chosen field. Are you the King or Queen of Monster.com? Do you find yourself scouring Craigslist for hours? It's probably wasted time.

In fact, while on a career leadership panel addressing university students entering the job market, I joked about the topic. I told them, "The good news for the seniors out there is, I'm telling you for every day you spend updating your résumé and applying for jobs online, you should spend four days partying."

Note: I could go into much greater detail about effective job search techniques, but remember this book is focused on salary negotiation, so I am assuming you're at or close to that point in the interviewing process already.

How will a strong network help you out during salary negotiations? By making connections, you'll have an extended network you can reach out to in order to help you pinpoint the salary range for jobs you are applying for.

However, when trying to determine salary ranges from your network, you have to utilize your connections carefully. The last thing anyone wants is an e-mail asking how much money they make from someone with whom they are loosely connected, so you have to tread lightly. But I've found that when you sincerely ask people for advice, they are more than happy to assist you.

You should tailor your conversation based on how well you know the person. In general I tend to be overappreciative and humble in my initial request. If connecting with someone via e-mail, you might consider writing something like this:

```
Hi John,

How are you? I am a friend of Jane Smith from ABC Company, and I believe we
met in person at her friend Joe's birthday party in November. I remember speak-
ing with you about your work at National Publishing.

I am currently looking for new work opportunities, and have a second interview
for a Senior Editor position at Pub Corp next week. I have done much research
in preparation for the interview, but was wondering if I could ask your opinion
on one area.

In your experience, what would the average salary range be for this position?
If you're not comfortable speaking on this topic, simply let me know. I'm not
looking for anything that is confidential to you or your company, but a ballpark
range would help reaffirm my analysis that I'm targeting the right compensation
during my negotiations.

Note that the Senior Editor reports to the Editor-in-Chief and manages a team
of three, and that I have 10 years of experience working in the industry.

Thank you in advance for your assistance.

Sincerely,

Jim Hopkinson
```

A simple e-mail like that could go a long way to determining your target range. If John is unwilling or unable to help, thank him for his time and ask if he knows anyone who could better assist you.

Who are some people or organizations you can reach out to?

- Put out the word to family, friends, and friends of friends who can help you target someone in the industry.

- Speak to your past and current mentors. (You *do* have a mentor, right?)

- Look for industry events on sites like Meetup.com. In some cases, you may actually be more comfortable asking a complete stranger you just met about the range, as there is less pressure without a personal connection.

- Attend a job fair for your industry. In a best-case scenario, often in a large city where there is unemployment in a particular sector, you may be able to go to a large expo where you could move from table to table and get opinions from many people in less than an hour.
- Contact your college career department or alumni group. It is in their best interest to have all their graduates happily employed, and they will have industry data to share with you.
- Contact some outplacement counselors, recruiters, and headhunters to see what kind of information you can get from them.

When receiving advice on the salary range, remember to tailor it to your specific situation.

Remember to account for:

- Number of years of experience
- Special skills that you bring
- Management experience
- Number of people you'd be managing
- Advanced degrees you hold
- Whether you're in a booming or a declining industry
- Size of company
- Part of the country you're in

Here's a personal story that shows how I used a combination of online research, social media, following my passion, and personal networking to help me gain an advantage for the job at *Wired*.

First, I knew I wanted to work for a cool company based in Manhattan that was producing new media content around a topic that I was passionate about, so I started examining the websites and products that I used every day. For example, I'm a runner and subscribe to *Runner's World* magazine. I ended up making a connection with a Sales Rep at their parent company, Rodale. They were able to connect me with the right person to talk to, but after exchanging a few e-mails, we determined there weren't any open jobs that fit my skill set at that time.

Then, I started looking at anything around the house that I enjoyed, be it my mountain bike or one of my tech gadgets, and started researching the parent companies or their marketing. I own three Specialized bicycles and they had a few cool-sounding jobs on their website, but their headquarters was located in California.

Finally, I sat down on my couch to think and looked over and saw my copy of *Wired* magazine sitting on my coffee table. I had been a subscriber for several years, and I really enjoyed their mix of technology and culture. I immediately jumped on the computer and found out that while the editorial staff was based in San Francisco, their parent company, Condé Nast, was based in New York, and that was where all the sales and marketing staff were located. I checked their job site and found a position that wasn't quite the perfect fit but looked very interesting. I spent a great deal of time doing more research, writing the perfect cover letter, and customizing my résumé to the position. Then I sent it in through their online application system.

If I had gotten a response the next day inviting me in for an interview, that would certainly be a great success story, wouldn't it? But that's not how it works. I knew that I would be competing with dozens, if not hundreds, of other résumés, so I started digging to find a connection to someone at *Wired*.

At the time, I probably had three hundred connections on LinkedIn, built from friends and coworkers in Boston, Seattle, and New York. That was a lot to go through, so I started with my friends who had the most connections, figuring they were the most "dialed in." One former ESPN colleague had about four hundred connections, so I paged through every one of them, but nothing jumped out.

My friend Matt also had more than four hundred connections, so I started analyzing those. The problem was, Matt was based in Boston, so I found page after page of people from that area. I was ready to move on, but the very next page was like finding gold at the bottom of a river. A woman named Laura, one of Matt's connections, worked for *Wired* in New York.

I immediately wrote to him, and although we hadn't spoken in a few years, as former fraternity brothers we quickly jumped on the phone and started rehashing old times. We caught up on careers, family, and friends, and he told me how he had worked with Laura at Lycos, the Massachusetts-based company that owned Wired.com before Condé Nast acquired it.

The next step was Matt reaching out to Laura, and before I knew it I had a person on the inside hand-delivering my résumé to the hiring manager.

Step 3: Preparing your "IRS document"

Just reading the three letters "IRS" is enough to cause some people to break into a cold sweat. And why not? It seems the sole purpose of the Internal Revenue Service is to *take* as much of your hard-earned money *away* from you as they can.

But for the Salary Tutor, IRS stands for "Industry Research of Salaries," and is a document you'll create with the goal of *bringing in* as much revenue as possible. Let's look at how to create your IRS document.

By now, you should have a very solid range in mind based on the following:

- How much you are making now
- What your skills are worth in the workplace
- What the range is for your industry

You should also have a number based on:

- The *lowest* figure you would accept
- The most likely *range* you'll be negotiating
- A *goal number* that you'd really like to hit if you do exceptionally well preparing for this interview

	Current					Best case negotiation	
				Target salary			
		Targeted range based on research					
		Lowest I'd Accept					
$50,000	$55,000	$60,000	$65,000	$70,000	$75,000	$80,000	

Image: Jim Hopkinson/Erin Fitzsimmons

For example, your thought process might be something like this:

- I'm making $55,000 per year now, and while my job is okay, I am ready for a change and I know that I could be making more money.
- In order to uproot everything and go to a new job, even if it's a really great opportunity, I'd need at least a 10 percent raise. The bottom figure I would accept is $60,000.
- Based on my research both online and within my personal network, I know positions for someone with my skill set make roughly between $60,000 and $70,000, depending on the job.
- Since I just completed some specialized training in my field and have more management experience than some of my peers, I am targeting the top end of that range, closer to $70,000.
- Because I now know from this book that the average candidate doesn't do this type of preparation and might sell themselves short in terms of salary, if I am confident in my abilities, present my research, and nail this interview, a target goal of $75,000 is attainable.

So, now that you know the salary range of the job you're going for, you should present this data to the HR person in your interview, right?

Not yet. First I'm going to show you how to organize it.

Go back to the following sites:

- Salary.com
- Payscale.com
- Glassdoor.com

We're going to create the IRS document to illustrate the salary research and analysis we've done in the industry. To do so, enter your geographical location and the name of the job title that you are interviewing for (if there's not an exact match, try a few different ones). The site might ask you additional questions about your education, experience, and so forth. After filling out all the information, you'll eventually get a graph and data showing you the salary range for that position.

There are a few paths you can take when deciding how to display this information to the person you are interviewing with, depending on your design skills.

The easiest way to present this information is to just print out the pages from whatever salary site you are using directly to your printer. It's fast, all the data is there, and you just have to click File, then Print.

However, when simply printing a web page, it's not always a clean process. Sometimes it prints on multiple pages, it doesn't format correctly, or it contains a lot of distracting information such as ad banners, promotions, navigation, and so on. You want the interviewer to focus on only the data that is relevant.

I suggest pulling together all of your salary research data and really adding some creativity to the design of your document. Rather than simply printing an existing webpage, custom design your own document in an "infographic-style" look, adding elements of color, unique icons, and summary bullet points about your skills, this position, and additional supporting data to back up your numbers. For example, sources you might list could include the Bureau of Labor Statistics, colleagues in the industry, and tech recruiters that helped you target the salary range for this job.

It could appear like this:

If you are not familiar with Photoshop or other design programs, you should ask someone to help you. Even if you have to pay someone a small fee or

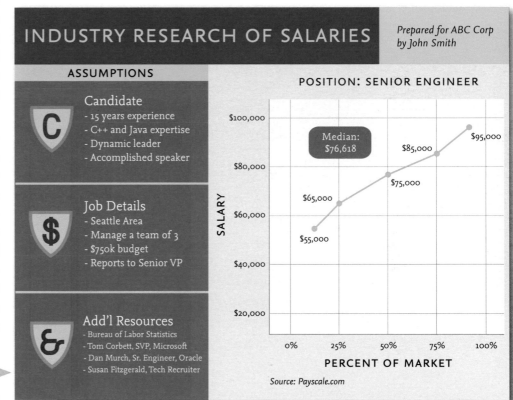

INDUSTRY RESEARCH OF SALARIES

Prepared for ABC Corp by John Smith

ASSUMPTIONS

C Candidate
- 15 years experience
- C++ and Java expertise
- Dynamic leader
- Accomplished speaker

$ Job Details
- Seattle Area
- Manage a team of 3
- $750k budget
- Reports to Senior VP

& Add'l Resources
- Bureau of Labor Statistics
- Tom Corbett, SVP, Microsoft
- Dan Murch, Sr. Engineer, Oracle
- Susan Fitzgerald, Tech Recruiter

POSITION: SENIOR ENGINEER

Median: $76,618

$100,000 — $95,000
$85,000
$80,000 — $75,000
$65,000
$60,000
$55,000
$40,000
$20,000

SALARY

0%   25%   50%   75%   100%
PERCENT OF MARKET

Source: Payscale.com

Image: Jim Hopkinson/Erin Fitzsimmons

offer to take them to lunch, you will be paid back ten times over if this document helps you secure a few thousand dollars more a year.

Another way to display your IRS document would be to present your completed design digitally on a tablet such as the Apple iPad.

No matter which design approach you take, your final IRS document will be a compelling resource guide to have with you during your interview.

Think about this for a second.

How many job candidates do you think are walking into an interview with a well-designed salary analysis document customized to the position and industry? My guess is less than 10 percent.

If I were the hiring manager, and someone I was interviewing came to me with a document like this and presented it at the proper time, I'd say the foresight, analysis, presentation, and preparedness alone would be enough to give them the bump in salary they were asking for.

But what if your range doesn't match up with theirs?

Don't worry. I have a plan for that.

Consider the following scenario:

Let's say that you have a rather broad title, such as Product Manager. The salaries vary widely depending on the industry, experience, and skills needed for a particular position. All of your research says that the job is definitely going to pay in the $50,000–$100,000 range. After doing additional research both online and with your contacts, you predict that the job you are interviewing for will most likely be in the $70,000–$75,000 range.

However, you don't want to create a graph that is $10,000 too high or too low. The solution?

Create three different IRS documents.

Okay, I can hear the groaning from everyone right now. Three times the work? Why go through all that effort?

Really? You're going to argue with me on this one?

First of all, you're only applying for dream jobs that you really love, right?

Second, you need to create this document only when you're going on an actual interview and you feel that an offer is coming.

Third, this should take you or your designer only an extra hour at most to complete, and once you have created the template for one job, you can reuse it for future interviews.

The point is this: You are going into a negotiation where every extra effort you make will distinguish you from the competition and could net you thousands of dollars. For the sake of argument, let's say it takes an extra *eight hours* to create this document and you had to pay a designer friend *$137* to do it. If it helps you get the job, the return on investment for the money spent would be the equivalent of exactly *one workday* based on a job paying $50,000 per year.

So what you would do for the job I just described is to adjust the graphs in your IRS document to show the following ranges:

- $50,000–$70,000
- $65,000–$85,000
- $75,000–$95,000

What factors would you adjust for? Think about the variables in the job you are interviewing for.

Perhaps you will be managing four people, not two like the job posting originally said. Perhaps during the interview they decide that you would be a better Project Manager versus Product Manager. Perhaps you find out that they are changing their publishing system over to WordPress, and you are an expert in WordPress. Perhaps the company just came off their best year, and their budgets have been increased (or maybe the opposite is true).

Bottom line: A number of variables could present themselves during the hiring process that could cause the pay for the job to fluctuate thousands of dollars in either direction. You want to be prepared for any of them.

What you should do next is have three different folders in the bag or portfolio that you bring to the interview. You should mark them in such a way that *you* know which folders contain the low, medium, and high ranges, but the interviewer should not be able to tell.

Example scenario

Your research says that the broad range of the job is $50,000–$100,000, and most likely within $70,000–$75,000.

Create three folders, each with a different set of graphs:

Low:	$50,000–$70,000
Medium:	$65,000–$85,000
High:	$75,000–$95,000

Okay, assuming this is done, is now the time that you are ready to unload all your salary history knowledge and your glorious IRS document?

Not yet.

In fact…quite the opposite. Put those documents aside for later, and read on.

Step 4: Don't get eliminated

The rule here is:

You should defer all specific salary talk until you know that they want you for the job.

Of course, this goal is completely counter to what the employer is trying to do, so it isn't going to be easy.

It's going to take a mix of preparedness, resolve, intelligence, and personality to pull it off.

Why do employers want to know your previous salary as quickly as possible?

- Companies get hundreds of résumés for a position.
- Your previous salary can be used to gauge your level of experience.
- Salary range is a quick and easy way for companies to judge and eliminate candidates.

Your goal is not to get eliminated.

To be clear, your specific, tactical goal during the interviewing process is to not reveal your current salary or give a specific range until the following two things have happened:

1. You've come to the point where you know that they are very interested in you for the position.
2. You've made them give their range first.

Again, companies are going to try to screen you out as soon as possible. The level of screening that is done will vary greatly depending on the company and the position.

For a smaller business, the hiring process might be very casual. Here's how it worked at my start-up: For this business, there were only three tiers of employees. There were four experienced founding partners, consisting of the CEO, VP/Development, VP/Sales, and VP/Marketing. At the next level were three managers in their mid- to late twenties. Finally, there were several developers, designers, video editors, and QA technicians all in their early twenties, just starting out their careers.

One of the partners would tell me that we needed to hire a new QA person, and the job opening would be advertised or spread via word of mouth. Soon after, the résumés would come pouring in. Even though I had no formal HR or interviewing experience, they quickly saw that I had a knack for filtering through résumés, picking out the gems, and narrowing down the potential hires.

Only after the three managers agreed on the finalists did we pass the person on to the partners. Because they wanted to keep the financials of the business private, they were the ones who talked to the candidates about salary. This would usually happen in a second or third interview.

Once a company is large enough to have a human resources department, things change pretty quickly.

While recent software and services allow companies to automate or outsource tasks such as payroll, benefits, and employee policies, once a company reaches fifty employees it usually gets to be too much for one person to handle on the side. At this point, the hiring process generally becomes more structured as well.

Larger companies mean more employee turnover and more jobs that need to be filled, and as a company's visibility grows that could mean hundreds of résumés pouring in daily that have to be filtered.

When this happens, it's logical to start eliminating candidates using salary range. Think of it in your own life. If you've recently decided that you need to purchase a brand-new car, there are hundreds of models to choose from. It would take weeks to test-drive every single one.

But if you know right off the bat that your budget is in the $20,000–$30,000 range, you can quickly eliminate an entire class of cars from Audi, BMW, and Porsche that retail in the $30,000-and-up category. Although, boy, it is still fun to sit in them and dream, right?

So in contrast to the small business, where you might not discuss salary until you meet with the CEO during the third round of interviews, with a large company you might face the question on a job application while you are sitting in the human resources waiting room.

If you are faced with this situation, then my recommendation is to avoid answering the question directly.

What if they ask for previous salary on the application?

- Leave it blank.
- Write "competitive." • ➤

What if they ask for desired salary on the application?

- Leave it blank.
- Write "negotiable." • ➤
- Write "to be discussed."

You might be asking if not filling this out completely will work against you. Let's look at the scenarios.

Previous Employer:	ABC Corp
Previous Salary:	$ Competitive

Position Desired:	Senior Manager
Desired Salary:	$ Negotiable

- You could be filling out a generic application form that is mostly intended to get your personal information and brief work experience. Maybe they don't even use the salary range prominently in their screening process, so if you don't answer directly it's no big deal. But if you put in a number that is too high or too low, you're giving them a reason to eliminate you.
- What if you're answering an ad with an intimidating footer in all caps that says, "APPLICATIONS THAT DO NOT INCLUDE FULL SALARY HISTORY WILL BE DISCARDED AND NOT CONSIDERED." Well, what does that tell you about the company? A great company wants to hire the best people at a mutually beneficial rate, and starting off like this raises a red flag for me.
- Last, you want to avoid this scenario in the first place. Remember that 80 percent of jobs are secured through networking. If you have a connection at the company, you can often bypass HR completely. Or if you feel you *must* put a figure, your research will at least get you to the range where you will not be eliminated—but you should still avoid it.

Step 5: Navigating the first interview

Okay, you've sidestepped the salary question on the job application, and now you're in your first interview with HR or one of the managers.

When it comes to salary, we're going to focus on:

- When to bring it up
- Who brings it up
- Who answers first

When to bring it up

To repeat what I wrote earlier, the optimal time to discuss salary is once they know they want you for the job. There must be a certain level of interest.

Who brings it up

As a job seeker, you should never be the person who brings up salary first. Although it would seem logical that compensation is just one more factor about the job, lumped in with questions about the hours, responsibilities, dress code, amount of travel, and management style, I think the impression still remains that a candidate who brings up money first can be perceived as greedy.

When giving job-search advice to people, I tell them that they need to view the interview process as a two-way conversation. There is a specific mind-set that you have to adopt, and many people are not comfortable with it until they are older and have more experience.

For this book, let's call this the Master Mind-set. Let me explain what I mean. Since you are the one seeking the job, and the person you are speaking with may eventually be your boss, it is natural that you feel as if the interviewer is the master and you are the student. You need to prepare thoroughly in order to impress the interviewer, you want to be ready for any questions they have, and you want to prove to them that they should hire you.

However, when you think in terms of the Master Mind-set, you realize that *you* are an extremely valuable asset as well. As much as you need to impress *them*, they need to also convince *you* that this is a great place to work and that you will be appreciated. After all, you're the one who will be dedicating thousands of hours of your hard work to making them successful. Most people are concerned only with answering the interviewer's questions, when ideally the interviewee should also hit them right back with equally challenging questions about the company's goals, product line, and management team.

In other words, don't view it as a Master and Student situation, but rather Master versus Master. The interviewer is the master of this company, and they know what the job entails, which person would be the best fit, and how much they will pay someone to perform that job. Meanwhile, you are the master of your own career. You know the tasks that you enjoy doing, what type of organization is the best fit for your personality, and how much your skills are worth in the industry.

Note that there's a right way and a wrong way to hit them right back. I instruct people to show initiative and take control of the second half of the interview through the use of a personal portfolio, and *only after asking* if you may show some examples.

In fact, I think a personal portfolio is an underutilized "secret weapon" that every individual should have, not just designers, photographers, and other creative types. I feel that savvy job-seekers in just about any industry can assemble a professional-looking portfolio of compelling documents that illustrate what would make them a superior employee.

Further, with the emergence of tablet devices like the Apple iPad, you have another option for easily displaying both examples of your work and your IRS document. Go to SalaryTutor.com for more information about creating an effective personal portfolio.

At the end of the interview, the scorecard should read 60 percent for the interviewer and 40 percent for the job seeker in terms of taking control and asking questions. However, "How much will I be paid?" is the one question that a job seeker should *not* bring up.

Who answers first

Put simply, for the most leverage during negotiation, the job seeker should never be the one who states a figure first. Knowing that the salary discussion should not be brought up until you know you are a top candidate for a position, what happens when you're still in the first interview and the interviewer asks?

Answer: You're going to have to find a way to defer the question until later in the interviewing process.

This is not an easy task, but there are responses that you can practice to make it happen. Before I tell you what they are, I want to make two points:

1. Every situation is going to be different. Only you know your own personality. Are you an outgoing salesperson who can charm people within minutes of meeting them? Or are you a shy bookworm who just wants a new job in accounting? You are going to have to tailor your response accordingly.

2. I'm going to talk again about the Master Mind-set. There are many job seekers who get to this stage of an interview and simply have no idea what to say. By learning my techniques, you will no longer fit in this category. Of the people who are reading this, many will simply *memorize* the tips and tricks and know *what* to say. This will give them a leg up on the competition. The proper mind-set, however, is to truly *understand* this information. Don't treat it as a secret trick to repeat back to the interviewer, but rather internalize and *believe what you are saying*.

© iStockphoto.com/LisaGagne

Confused? Let me give you a personal example.

My first job was doing technical support for a software company. Yes, it's exactly what you're thinking. I was one of a few dozen tech geeks lined up side by side in a cubicle farm in Cambridge, Massachusetts. We were all wearing those dorky headsets, answering call after call (more than ten thousand total in my eighteen months there) from people complaining about one issue or another with their software.

Within a year, I was a manager who helped train the new reps. You know when they say, "This call might be monitored for training purposes"? I was the monitor.

During training, both the new employee and I would have our headsets connected to the same call in order to listen, but I would be on mute so that the caller could not hear me. I soon realized that there were three types of employees:

1. Employees who didn't know anything

This was basically everyone during their first few weeks on the job. This employee might seem to be an unbelievable über-geek upon hire but couldn't know the ins and outs of the software until the job actually began. That was where the training came in.

2. Employees who were able to repeat steps to correct a specific problem

To be honest, the first time you take a call on your own, it can be terrifying. You pray that the question is about the software program you are most familiar with (I think we had more than a dozen), and that the call is about a known problem.

For example, if someone was calling and said that they were trying to print mailing labels on Avery 5280 three-by-four-inch stickers and couldn't line them up correctly, this was a known problem and you simply told them to choose template #5 and set the right margin to 0.6 inches and that should correct it. These employees *know what to say*, but they are just *repeating* something someone has told them.

3. Employees who believed what they were saying

This is usually illustrated by a veteran call rep kicking back in his chair with his feet on his desk, taking call after call, without having to consult his notes.

Not every person made it to level 3.

I specifically remember shadowing an employee named Kevin. A call came in and the person simply said, "My document isn't printing." He put the person on hold, looked at me frantically, and I told him to ask the customer to go to File, choose Printer Setup, and tell him what printer he had selected.

He got back on the phone and said exactly what I told him word for word: "Um, yes sir, can you click on File, choose Printer Setup, and tell me what printer you have selected?" The caller gave a two-word answer: "HP Deskjet."

Once again, Kevin looked at me frantically. He put the caller on hold again, and asked what to do next. This went on for ten minutes, as he could only repeat what I told him, not truly grasp the bigger picture and believe what he was saying in trying to correct the problem. He was let go within two weeks.

Remember the Master Mind-set as we talk about our responses to the salary question. Don't just regurgitate the lines that I am telling you, but actually make them your own and believe in them.

There are two main ways that an interviewer might pose a question about salary:

1. What is your *desired* salary?
2. What is your current or *previous* salary?

For the first method, the question might be brought up casually.

> Evil HR Lady: "So...how much money are you looking to make here?"

A good response that will allow you to defer the salary discussion could be:

> "Well, to be honest, I think it might be a little bit early in the process for me to try to pinpoint a specific number.

> "I think I have a general feel for the job based on what we've talked about so far, but if we both decide to move forward, I'd really like to speak to the other people I'd be working with and have a greater understanding of everything involved before getting into a salary discussion. Would that be okay?"

This is where the Master Mind-set comes in.

Yes, you can memorize those lines, but sit back and think about this honestly for a moment.

You've just been talking to an HR representative for fifteen minutes. *How can you honestly judge how much money you should be making until you know everything about the position?*

What if you say something on the lower end of your range, and then you find out that there is more travel than expected, the operating budget is half of what you're used to, or that you don't have the design resources needed to get the job done efficiently?

You might like other things about the job, but suddenly you're thinking, *Wow, I'd really need to be making an extra $10,000 a year to make this job worthwhile.*

Or what if you state your range on the higher side, but continue the interviewing process, only to find that this is your dream job? You click instantly with your would-be manager and the rest of the team, you find out that there's a new project in the pipeline that you'd kill to work on, and that there are performance bonuses. You'd practically take a pay cut for this opportunity.

Alas, you gave a high number to the person in HR who has no connection to this group, and you are screened out and passed over for a less expensive candidate.

Thus, try to change your mind-set to honestly saying and believing,

> "I really don't know what the perfect salary is until I know everything about the job."

Okay, so the Evil HR Lady listens intently to your initial response, but she really wants a number. She counters with the following statement:

> "Well, I understand that you want to know more about the position from the other staff, but I don't want to waste anyone's time going through that process if we're too far apart with numbers. Can you at least give me a range of what you're looking for?"

This is where your heart starts to race, but it's even more important now to hold your ground. Your response could be:

> "Well, I've actually done a fair amount of research while preparing for this interview, which I'd be happy to share with you later if we both decide there's a good fit here.

> "What I found is that there was a pretty wide range depending on a number of factors, and I'd really need to have the full picture of all the responsibilities before I know what that range is."

Again, this is the honest truth. You *have* done a significant amount of research, and you have seen how easy it is for the range to slide $10,000 in either direction depending on the skills needed and the industry. Hold your ground.

One way to try to sidestep the question is to give your answer and then change the subject.

For example...

> "You know, in preparing my research for this interview, it really became clear to me that the salary range could vary widely based on specific responsibilities, for example, the size of the budget for the department I'd be managing. With the economy the way that it's been, would you say the budget for this group has grown, shrunk, or stayed the same, and how does that affect the ability to get projects done?"

And another...

> "I understand that making sure we're in the same salary range is important, and I've done my research to find out what the rough range for this position is.
>
> "But what was interesting was that as I was researching the analytical data, I came across several studies relating salary to job satisfaction, and what was really important was a great boss, a supportive team, and having a fun atmosphere.
>
> "So I pledged to make sure to really pay attention to the culture here, and knew that the money side would work itself out when the time came. So maybe you can talk a little more about the culture."

The second way the salary question could be posed to you is by asking about your *previous* salary.

> "So...how much were you making at your last job?"

Or they could call you out on the job application if you left it blank:

> "I noticed you didn't fill out the salary history section on the job application. We need that information to move forward."

Again, tailor your response to your situation. If you are currently unemployed, many people do some side work and call themselves a consultant. Use this to your advantage.

Scenario 1

You were making a high relative wage while consulting. For example, you got $100 to tutor some students for a one-hour class, or did a freelance design job for $1,000 that took you ten hours. In both cases, your salary was $100/hour. You could say:

> "Well, the reason I didn't list my previous salary on the application is that I've been freelancing since I was laid off, and the compensation for that would equal $200,000 if you calculated it out annually.
>
> "I've done my homework regarding a full-time position in this industry and know the general range, so I don't think we'll have any problems discussing it when it's time for the next step in the process."

Scenario 2

You were making a low relative wage while consulting. For example, your friend gave you $100 to help them build a website or you took a retail job to earn money. Your answer could be:

> "The reason I didn't state my salary from my last position is that I used the time off to help some friends start a business. Therefore, what I was making on those projects wasn't a true reflection of my worth. What I'm most interested in now is hearing more about this position to make sure it's a good fit for both of us."

What if they keep pushing you?

They ask how much you were making at your last job, and your first attempt to defer the conversation got a smile and a nod. But then they come back again and say:

> "I'm happy to tell you all about the position, but before I can pass you off to the hiring manager, I really need to know how much you're making now."

Do you have to tell them?

Nick Corcodilos is a former headhunter who runs a very informative, no-nonsense site called AskThe Headhunter.com. He's answered over 30,000 questions about job hunting and hiring since 1995, and on the topic of salary, he states:

> "There is no law that says you have to divulge your past salary, or that you must allow your future income to be limited by your past income." He goes on to say that there are two reasons you should never divulge your salary:
>
> - "The first is that it's private and no one's business. It's confidential. Any company should be ashamed of itself for prying so insistently into your finances, and embarrassed to admit that it seeks to determine your value through the judgments of other companies, rather than to evaluate and judge you for itself."
> - "The second reason you should not divulge your salary is more important. The minute you open your kimono and expose your salary, any negotiating leverage you have disappears with your modesty. The employer now has the edge."

So what's a good way to answer the question? One of Nick's readers came up with this fantastic line of logic:

If you are currently employed by a major company, you probably were issued an employee policy handbook, or you signed some form of employment contract when you were hired. Within this agreement, there is most likely a firm policy regarding the distribution of confidential company information.

It usually includes rules such as:

- You can't use work computers for personal use.
- You can't leverage company products for your own advantage.
- You can't work with your company's competitors.
- You cannot share sensitive company information with the public.

Take a look at that last bullet point. Whether it is spelled out specifically or not, this can be interpreted that you cannot share compensation data publicly. Think about what would happen if you were a manager

© iStockphoto.com/jtyler

and posted the salaries of every worker in your department on Facebook. I doubt you would be working there much longer.

Considering that most people stay roughly within the same industry, and thus the new job you are applying for could be viewed as a competitor, I think the following response is completely valid:

> "How much am I making now? I'm sorry, but the employment contract that I'm under with my current employer does not allow me to reveal my compensation. However, I'm sure that when the time comes to discuss salary, we won't have a problem settling on a number we can both agree on."

A friend of mine actually used a similar tactic recently without even knowing it. There are only three or four well-established companies in her industry, and they were very competitive for talent. Knowing what the other companies were paying their key staff would be a huge advantage. Her genuine response to the question was as follows:

> "Well, as you know, the nonprofit arena is a very small, very tight-knit community. I'm sure my current employer would not be pleased if I were to tell competitors what their employees were getting in terms of compensation, so I don't feel comfortable revealing that information."

Here is another way to answer that question, especially if you're changing careers.

> "You know, I really think my last job was a unique situation. I wanted to gain on-the-job knowledge and break into this field, so I was fine with working a little bit below what the market was probably paying.

> "So I'm not sure if there's a direct correlation between what I was making there and what my value would be at this current position. I'd like to keep learning more about what the responsibilities here would be."

This response takes the economic conditions of 2009–2010 into consideration:

> "You know, I started at my last job in 2006, and it was a really different time compared to now. I know some companies are still doing well, but a lot of them have really been affected by the economy.

"So I think it's really hard to compare what I was making then with a similar position now. If we decide we're a good fit, I'm curious to see what range you have for this position."

It's understandable that a job seeker would be hesitant to challenge the interviewer. They are holding the key to your future at this company, so to avoid a direct question would seem to put you at a disadvantage.

But I am proof that holding your ground can work.

At the end of our first meeting, the HR rep finished up by asking, "So...how much were you making at your last job?"

I used one of the scenarios above to defer the topic.

She followed up again, asking, "I really need to know what your range is."

Although I was nervous and really wanted to cave, I had prepared myself for this pressure, and I was able to politely defer the topic again.

At this point the HR rep sat back in her chair, smiled, and said to me, "You're not going to tell me what you made at your last position, are you?"

I smiled back and shook my head no.

As the interview ended, and she reflected on my research of the company, my knowledge of the industry, my portfolio, the answers I gave, and the questions I asked, capped off with the proper salary response, she told me, "You might be the most prepared candidate I've ever seen."

So not only did I not *anger* the interviewer, I *impressed* her.

Tutor
Test 3

Take a few moments to write out and practice the defer tactic that you will use for your specific situation.

_____

_____

_____

_____

_____

_____

_____

_____

_____

_____

_____

Step 6: The no-win question

Okay, you've met with the rest of the staff, you have a full understanding of the job and all of its responsibilities, and you now find yourself back in human resources, or speaking with an executive who will be making the hiring decision.

© iStockphoto.com/moodville

What do you do when it *is* time to talk salary?

In my experience, this all comes down to a serious game of "verbal chicken." That is, who is going to blink first? You? Or the Evil HR lady? Somebody has to put a salary number on the table to get the game started, and ideally, you want her to start talking first. That's just basic common sense when it comes to negotiating, but for a lot of eager people, it's a step they don't recognize as being crucial in this process.

My recommendation: Use the "Right Back at Ya" Method, which we'll get to in a moment.

Again, this is going to take a little bit of resolve—and you can actually turn it into a fun exercise—but don't let your guard down just because you're on the cusp of getting the job. We need to keep our strategy going because, as we've learned, the best way to succeed in negotiation is to wait until you know they are very interested in offering you the job. Once that happens, the best strategy is to have the interviewer state their range first.

Let's look at the thinking behind this.

In some cases, the next step is easy. The company will come right out and let you know via letter or e-mail what their offer is.

In these cases, you are not under pressure to respond on the spot and can plot out your next step, which should be asking for an in-person meeting or a phone call to discuss your options.

If they inform you over the phone, you can say you need to think about it, and ask to return their call.

But most likely, they will make the salary offer in person.

When this happens, the easier path is that they come right out and tell you what they want to pay you. You can then proceed to the next steps, including showing them your research.

But the trickier path, usually presented by HR or more savvy negotiators, is that they revert to asking how much money you are looking to make.

In this case, one of two things can happen. Either you say a number first, or they do.

To this point, you have successfully avoided telling the HR department or the first round of screeners your current salary or your desired range. Some people think that now is the time to take the initiative and state your salary demands. Do you?

The recommendation is still no. The best way to succeed in negotiations is to have the interviewer state their number first. In other words, *whoever gives their number first has the most to lose.*

Let's look at the thinking behind this.

Let's say the budget for a position is $60,000 to $70,000.

Example 1

The question is posed: "So…how much money are you looking to make?"

You haven't done your research, so you nervously run through the one hundred responses that come to mind and blurt out the largest number you think they can handle, which is some combination of what your buddy told you to ask for, your current salary, plus a huge raise: "$80,000!"

Result?

If the interviewer had an "incorrect answer" game show buzzer, that's the sound that you would hear now. You overshot their range.

A few things can happen here:

- Maybe you can impress them *so* much that you beat out every other candidate and they decide to go back on their allocated budget number. But that outcome is probably not as likely.
- They quickly write you off as too expensive.
- They nod and complete the rest of the interview, but if it's between you and someone else, and that person will work for $68,000, they go with the other candidate.

The worst thing is, you could continue through the rest of the interview and find out that it was a really amazing job, one that you would have taken for just a small increase over your current rate, but you don't get it because you guessed over budget, and you never know the reason you didn't get the job.

Example 2

They ask, "How much are you looking to make?"

You haven't researched, and you're nervous and don't want to seem pushy, so you undervalue yourself and say, "I'd like to make $48,000."

The result here is that you chose a number well below their range.

A few scenarios could play out here, all of them bad:

- You could be immediately eliminated because they felt that your low salary meant that you weren't experienced enough for the job.
- They could actually give you the job at the $48,000 you asked for, and you'll never know that you're being underpaid by up to $22,000.
- The ultimate worst scenario: You take the job and work there for three years, and only *then* find out you've been making about 50 percent less than a coworker who negotiated well.

Example 3

They ask, "How much are you looking to make?"

You rear back, pick a random number out of your head, and decide on $65,000.

Bull's-eye, right? What's wrong with that?

True, you might get a job you want, at what you *think* is a fair salary. The downsides are:

- You could be in the running but might lose out to someone who negotiated better.
- Had you counteroffered, you could be making $5,000 more.

- You'll never know what the range was…and that can nag at you for months.
- You accept that range early in the interview, only to find out that there is a lot more to the job than you thought, but now it's tough to go back on it.

Let's go back to the Master Mind-set way of thinking.

The executive has asked you a direct question: How much money are you looking for?

I'm going to show you a few ways to reverse the question and put the ball back in their court, but it's more than just saying the lines, it's *believing* them.

Here's a simple way to think about it:

They are the ones offering the job.

- *They* know the need they have to fill, whether it's a marketing director or Java programmer or entry-level accountant.
- *They* are hiring someone because there is more work that can be accomplished, and in doing so they hope to bring in extra revenue.
- *They* know how much additional revenue can be generated, how much they pay their current employees, and what their budget limitations are.

So in your head (and not out loud), it's okay to say to yourself,

"Listen, Evil HR Lady, you're *the one with the open position here.* You *tell* me *how much it pays."*

© *iStockphoto.com/vitalijlang*

63

Step 7: The "Right Back at Ya" Method

When the question asking about your salary needs comes across the table, it might help to picture a tennis court. The executive is lobbing over a loaded question in an effort to get you aboard while paying you as little money as possible. But you're going to come right back at them with a question of your own about what they are willing to pay.

I call this the "Right Back at Ya" Method.

Your response will be in two parts.

1. You'll notice that the first part of your response might be very similar to your defer explanation, which we covered previously. You can use the exact same wording if you are negotiating with a new person, or if you find yourself back in front of the same Evil HR Lady, you can simply lead with, "Well, as I mentioned before…"

2. For the second part, you will turn the question back on the interviewer and ask what range they had budgeted for the position.

They serve: The interviewer asks something along the lines of:

> "So…how much were you looking to make in terms of salary?"

You return: The ball is now in your court, so answer back with an appropriate response.

THE GENERIC RESPONSE

> "Well, in preparing for this interview, I did some homework and found out the general range for a position like this, but it was clear to me that it could vary widely based on the company.
>
> "What type of range did you have budgeted for the position?"

THE ECONOMY RESPONSE

> "As you know, the last time I discussed starting salary for my last job was back in 2006, and it was a really different time compared to now.

What kind of salary were you looking for?

What range did you have budgeted for the position?

With the way the economy has been, I know some companies have done better than others at weathering the storm. While I've done my research, I know it varies from job to job.

"Based on the current environment, what type of range did you have budgeted for the position?"

THE FREELANCE RESPONSE

"Well, if I were to extrapolate the rate I'm getting from some of my freelance jobs over a year, I'd be asking for $200,000 or more.

"However, I know that's a bit high for this position, and I was wondering what type of range you have budgeted for the job."

THE CAREER CHANGER RESPONSE

"Well, as you know, I've been an assistant marketing manager for the last two years, but I am very excited about moving into event planning. As we discussed during my interview, I really think many of my skills will translate to this new field, but in doing my research, it was tough for me to pinpoint an exact salary range for my unique situation.

"So I'll ask you—what type of range did you have budgeted for this position?"

What if they push back?

A seasoned negotiator might return the volley back at you, saying something like:

"Well, our budget has some flexibility in it. Can you give me the range that you were looking for?"

Wipe the sweat from your brow because we have a real match on our hands. Stick to your guns and come back at them from another angle and ask again.

You might say:

"Well, I've done some research, and I clearly think that the skills that I would bring to this job will make it worth your while, but you're in the best position to determine what a company like yours values for a position like this. What kind of range is ABC Corp. comfortable with?"

If they keep pressing harder, or you sense that the interviewer is legitimately getting angry and that the only way out is to give a number, then you should use what I call the Crazy Range.

It's basically the same phrase, but with some numbers in there. Let's assume that you feel the job is in the $75,000 range. It goes something like this:

> "Based on my research, the salary range for a position like this varies greatly depending on the company, the responsibilities, and the experience of the candidate…paying anywhere from $50,000 up to $100,000 or more.
>
> "What type of range does ABC Corp. have budgeted for this particular job?"

What did you just do there?

- They asked for numbers, and you gave them some.
- You showed that you've done some research.
- You said your salary range is effectively $50,000 to $5 million.
- You put the ball back in their court.

The risk here is that they'll assume $50,000 would be the lowest number you would take. But it's all in the delivery and attitude.

You're definitely not saying something direct, such as "Well, the lowest I would accept is $50,000, but I've seen salaries that are higher than that."

When you're giving the crazy range, you're talking about the market for *this job*, not your *personal market*.

Let's imagine that someone was trying to sell me a one-bedroom apartment in New York City and asked how much I would pay. Adding a zero to the numbers in our example above, I'd reply, "Well, it depends greatly on the neighborhood, the building, and several other factors. I've seen cozy places on the Upper East Side for $500,000, and great places elsewhere for $1 million or more."

If you deliver the line emphasizing the vastness of range, they should get the picture. It's tough to describe in text (I guess you'll need to get the audio version of this book), but in the apartment example, it would be something like:

"Well [*pause; slight look of minor disbelief, as if you're searching for numbers, rolling your eyes a bit, while shrugging slightly and putting out your hands*], it depends greatly on the neighborhood, the building, whether there's a doorman [*counting things off on your fingers*], and several other factors. I've seen cozy places on the Upper East Side for $500,000 [*emphasizing this number as a low-end figure*], and great places elsewhere for $1 million or more [*raising voice slightly in a fun tone, almost filled with wonder*]."

By the way, for those of you unfamiliar with the New York real estate market wondering how a "cozy" one-bedroom apartment could cost half a million dollars, note that some might call that a *bargain*—data from residential brokerage firms Brown Harris Stevens and Halstead Property reported that the average Manhattan apartment sales price was $1,432,787 in the fourth quarter of 2010.

You've now swung your racket and hit a great return shot. What comes next?

Step 8: 30 seconds to glory

If all has gone according to plan, you've successfully lobbed the conversation back over the net, you've won the point, and the interviewer comes back to you with a number.

It's crunch time.

- This is the most difficult part of the entire process.
- This is the most painful.
- This is incredibly awkward.
- This is what you have to practice the most.

And this small thirty-second window is when you can potentially make the most money. Money that is not only going to be great starting the very first day you begin your job, but will also be the basis for subsequent raises, and even for other jobs after you've left this one.

What is the Master Mind-set for this? If you're a big fan of bank-robber movies, you could picture this not just as a salary negotiation but as a hostage negotiation.

If it helps to picture the Evil HR Lady as a crazed lunatic locked in a bank with ten hostages and explosives strapped to her body, so be it. Instead of her demanding millions of dollars and a private jet that is fueled and ready to go at a nearby airport, as she clutches bags of cash or diamonds, just picture her being very protective of the Excel spreadsheet that contains the total payroll budget for her company.

Your role is the wily FBI negotiator. Your goal is simply to make sure that at the end of the negotiation, no one gets shot, everyone is happy, and you get your fair share of that budget.

In doing my research, I came across an old FBI publication by Special Agent Gary W. Noesner, chief negotiator with the FBI's Critical Incident Response Group, and Dr. Mike Webster, a former member of the Royal Canadian Mounted Police, called "Crisis Intervention: Using Active Listening Skills in Negotiations."

They found that a growing number of law enforcement agencies had successfully used the following skills to effectively do their job.

Use FBI negotiation techniques to secure the highest salary.

Photo: Public Domain via Wikipedia

68

Seven techniques of active listening to bring a positive outcome in negotiations

1. **Minimal encouragements:** Demonstrate that you are listening attentively by repeating back simple words such as "Yes," "Okay," or "I see."

2. **Paraphrasing:** Repeat in your own words the meanings of the subjects' messages back to them, to show that you understand what they are saying.

3. **Emotion labeling:** Attach a tentative emotional label to a person (anger, stress, fear) to identify the issues that the person is feeling.

4. **Mirroring:** Similar to the first and second techniques, mirroring involves repeating back just the last few words that the other person has said.

5. **Open-ended questions:** Successful negotiators begin questions with "Tell me about…" as opposed to "Why…"

6. **"I" messages:** Use "I" in a crisis intervention to humanize the negotiator, making them a person as opposed to a law enforcement agent.

7. **Effective pauses:** Negotiators purposely leave gaps of silence in their conversation, as people tend to speak to fill the silence and may divulge important information in the process.

I'm going to show you how to use some of these FBI techniques in a moment, but first let's look at some other research that also recommends utilizing technique 7.

In her book *The Next Generation of Women Leaders: What You Need to Lead But Won't Learn in Business School*, author Selena Rezvani gives tips on using silence during negotiation, calling it "one of the greatest negotiation strategies at your disposal."

In her opinion, when used correctly, an uncomfortable silence can make the interviewer:

- Share information
- Restate their position
- Try to guess what your position is

All of these outcomes can have a positive effect on your level of salary.

As I pointed out in the beginning of the book, negotiation has historically been more difficult for women. Rezvani says, "The strategy of silence is especially important for women to use since they may be tempted to accommodate their counterpart, fill a conversation void, or not want to seem 'difficult' or 'withholding.'"

Okay, let's get back to the negotiating table and put these techniques into action.

Your "Right Back at Ya" statement is:

> "What type of range did you have budgeted for the position?"

The HR person takes the bait and responds with:

> "We've budgeted this position in the $65,000 to $75,000 range."

Respond by using techniques 1, 2, 4, and 7 from the FBI playbook (minimal encouragement, paraphrasing, mirroring, and effective pauses).

So your response would be something like:

> "I see. So you're saying that the top of your range is $75,000."

Then be silent.

By doing so, you've listened attentively, paraphrased what the interviewer has said, mirrored back the last few words (which, conveniently, is only the *top* number that she stated), and left an effective pause in the conversation to allow the interviewer to fill the gap.

In his excellent book on the subject, *Negotiating Salary: How to Make $1,000 a Minute*, author Jack Chapman simplifies the sentence down to just two words!:

- A number
- A four-letter word

What four-letter word do you think it is? I guess if you were expecting to make $30,000 and the interviewer said $75,000, you'd be ecstatic and those two words could be "$75,000? Damn!"

Or if you were expecting $100,000 and they offered $75,000, you'd be angry and those two words could be "Damn! $75,000?"

But no, Mr. Chapman did not become a well-known author and salary negotiation expert by encouraging profanity. His recommendation is:

1. Repeat the number at the top of the range.
2. Say the four-letter word "hmmm."
3. Then, use the silence technique.

So if the interviewer said:

> "We've budgeted this position in the $65,000 to $75,000 range."

Your response would be:

> "$75,000. Hmmm..." [*silence*]

What should your reaction and body language be during the silence?

Chapman says, "Your enthusiasm for the job and company and industry has been unbounded up to this point. Now let a quiet look of concern grace your countenance and gaze at your slightly shuffling feet as you ponder this offer."

What should your mind-set be?

There's a very good chance that you are learning about this silence trick for the first time. And to that end, you'll be nervous using it and want to break the silence yourself. But you need to stay focused and not say anything until the interviewer responds.

So what should you think about during those thirty seconds?

You should honestly think about what the next few months or years will be like working at this company at that salary. You've probably had a stressful, whirlwind process over the previous few weeks, writing cover letters, polishing your résumé, surviving a grueling interview process, and preparing for this moment.

It will be nice if you get the job, give your two-week notice at your old job, and head to Aruba for a week to clear your head before you start this new opportunity. •

Photo: Atilin via Wikipedia

But before your mind starts sipping piña coladas on the beach, give it a thirty-second gut-check and flash through everything that has happened:

- You've chosen a specific industry and company.
- You've networked to get this opportunity.
- You've impressed people in your interviews.
- You've implemented effective negotiation techniques.

Are you ready for *this* job in *this* industry at *this* salary?

By the time you've run through all that in your head, the thirty seconds are probably up.

But as you're doing that, hopefully—probably—the interviewer has broken the silence and responded. Most people hate awkward silence in conversation, and will rush to fill it. There are a few ways this could play out:

Upon your saying the number $75,000 and going silent, the person might respond with:

> "B-b-but but but…we might be able to go as high as $80,000."

Obviously that would be a great outcome.

You could start to nod your head, stay quiet, and keep thinking, and in the absolute best-case scenario, they might blurt out something like:

> "But to go any higher than that, we'd have to give you a higher title."

Hmmm, a better title. That's fine with me. Or they might move away from salary, but still try to sweeten the deal.

> "$80,000 is really our top end, but I might be able to get you three weeks' vacation to start instead of two."

Wow, a raise, a new title, and an extra week of vacation in less than five minutes. That would definitely be a fantastic best-case scenario. If you practice this technique until you are comfortable with it, then come across a less-experienced interviewer, the most likely outcome is going to be positive.

Before we look at other ways this could play out, here are two personal stories I will offer to show how a negotiation could unfold depending on the experience of those involved.

In the first, I was the one extending the offer. This was back when I was twenty-six years old, with no formal HR experience. I was working at the start-up, and to be honest, because we were really bootstrapping the company, it was a little embarrassing how little we were offering in terms of salary. When it came time to offer someone a position, I modeled it after a certain formula.

Have you heard the term *criticism sandwich*?

That's when you criticize someone's work, sandwiched between two compliments. So you might say, "John, I really liked the topic of your presentation today. If I could make one suggestion, I'd consolidate the section with all the corporate background to one or two slides to keep things moving. But overall I think you had great energy and held the attention of the audience." Your main point is to tell him to cut out the five boring slides about the corporate background in the middle, but to soften the blow by praising him about two other items that you liked.

In my scenario as the person delivering the offer, I didn't want to give the candidate the opportunity to challenge the low salary that we were offering, so I wedged it in between his title and his start date. It went like this:

"Hi, Joe. Thanks for coming in to interview this week. I have great news. We're offering you the position. Your title will be Application Developer reporting to me, your starting salary would be $24,000, and we'd like you start next Monday, the twenty-third."

I would then sit back and basically hold my breath. Usually people were just really excited to hear they got the job. I think there was only *one* person who ever challenged me on the salary, and I was so nervous that I basically said, "I'm not sure, I'm going to have to check," then ran to my VP to see what to do. I think if anyone had said, "I see...$24,000..." and then went deathly silent, I would have wet my pants.

On the flip side, I've heard of a situation where an extremely experienced business development executive locked horns with an extremely intelligent business owner during a huge negotiation.

The business owner told me, "We both knew what the other person was trying to do, and at one point, I think we both sat there staring at each other, neither of us breaking the silence, for what seemed like ten minutes." In the end, there was mutual respect between the two, and they were able to hammer out a very fair agreement.

Compliment

Criticism

Compliment

Photo: Public Domain via Wikipedia

You're probably thinking that the silence trick can't work in every situation, and you're correct. Often, your response will be met with something such as:

"I'm sorry, but because of the economy our budgets are really tight and that's all we can do."

Or they might say, "Were you expecting something higher than that?"

Or they could say, "Honestly, $75,000 is the maximum salary I have for this right now."

Each negotiation is different, and I could paint a number of different scenarios that could play out during your salary conversation with a prospective employer:

- They offer you a tiny bit more money than their original range.
- They come back with a number that is lower than you expected.
- They vastly exceed your salary expectations.
- They hold fast, citing budget concerns.
- Or things take a completely different turn…they say something that catches you completely by surprise, you yelled "Wow!" when you heard their number, or you started sneezing right when you were supposed to be quiet. Stranger things have happened.

Hang in there, because we're going to try one more thing.

Remember all that research you did at the beginning and put into the three folders? Now is the time to bust it out. No matter what the dollar figure is, I recommend you share your IRS document.

Why?

Remember that right now you are at your highest peak of negotiation leverage. *Your next salary review could be a year away.* Seize this opportunity during the few minutes that you have it. You might be asking yourself, *Shouldn't I be afraid that if I keep pushing for more money, they'll be offended or give the job to someone else?*

If you've handled yourself professionally and fairly up to this point, and you have waited until you're sure that you're one of the final candidates and they want you, you should be fine. The hiring manager knows that this is the time for back-and-forth, and although they want to save as much money as possible, what they *really* want is a happy employee. In the big picture, you are a huge investment in time and resources over the next few years, so why quibble over a few thousand dollars?

So let's take it from the top:

> Evil HR Lady: "What were you looking for in terms of salary?"
>
> You: "Based on my research, the salary range for a position like this varies greatly. What type of range did you have budgeted for the position?"
>
> HR: "Well, we've budgeted this position in the $60,000 to $70,000 range."
>
> You: "I see…$70,000…" [*silence*]
>
> HR: "Well, I'll need to talk to finance, but I might be able to get you $72,000. Would that be acceptable?"

So now the current offer on the table is $72,000. Look back at our three folders, which are labeled as follows:

> Low: $50,000–$70,000
> Medium: $65,000–$85,000
> High: $75,000–$95,000

You're already above the $70,000 mark, so you can eliminate the Low folder.

In general, companies might leave a few thousand dollars in wiggle room, but they're not going to give you an additional $25,000. So the folder in the High range with a top end of $95,000 is going to be way too high if their original range was $60,000–$70,000.

You'll want the middle one.

Your rehearsed response should be along the following lines:

"Well, I really appreciate the generous offer, and I'm really excited about the position. But I've done a lot of homework in preparation for this interview, and according to my analysis…

[reaching for chart]

"For this position, the typical salary range is between $65,000 and $85,000, with an average of $76,618.

"Based on all the responsibilities that we talked about:

- Managing a team of two
- Securing new business
- Traveling to the West Coast

"…and the fact that I have seven years of experience and my skill set will allow me to start contributing right away, I feel that I should be in the middle to high end of that scale.

"Is that something you can consider?"

You've now made one last articulate, rational, compelling argument for earning the maximum salary for your position, and you presented it in a thought-out, organized manner.

Referring to your salary analysis (IRS document) in this manner has a few advantages:

- First, since so few people will do this, it really sets you apart from the pack.
- Next, it shows you've done your homework and are not just throwing out numbers.
- Finally, if you are less comfortable socially or when thinking on the spot, it allows you to work from notes.

While you definitely want to keep a friendly, personable tone while doing this, referring to industry numbers makes the process seem more businesslike, as if the two of you are working together (I liken it to two people looking for directions on a map), as opposed to setting up a "you against me" scenario.

During this negotiation, watch closely how the interviewer responds, and think back to the FBI active listening skills. If they talk about how their budgets have been cut, try using paraphrasing and emotion labeling.

For example, if they say:

> "You know, I'd really like to do more for you, but they've really killed us on the budgets this year."

You could respond:

> "Wow, I can understand about the budgets. It sounds like it's been really frustrating this year."

Hopefully this empathy and commiserating with their restrictive budgets will help soften up the interviewer, making him or her open up a bit and want to help you. I mean, what manager has the problem of having *too much* money in the budget?

As an aside, as you're heading out on that final vacation before you start your new job, this is also a good travel technique. If I'm looking to get an upgrade on a flight or move from a middle seat to the window, I always approach the person at the desk with a smile and shake my head and say, "Wow, I bet you've had a crazy day today." I don't think I've ever had someone respond by saying things were actually quite calm. *Of course* the attendants at the airport have had a crazy day! With flight delays, security concerns, and people all trying to board at once, every flight has a little bit of chaos. By commiserating with them, you've got a much better chance at that window seat than the pushy jerk who is chewing them out because it's snowing in St. Louis.

The second active listening technique is to keep asking open-ended questions. You never want to be confrontational and say something like "I know plenty of Product Managers who make $80,000 and I have more skills than any of them!" Instead, you want to keep referring back to the range and emphasizing your skills.

For example:

> "$72,000 is a generous offer, but as you can see, this range is pretty broad. On the low end of $65,000, I'm assuming those are for project managers with a little less experience, or in a less expensive part of the country, while $85,000 is the maximum reported.
>
> "But remember that I already have my PMP certification, and I would be managing a staff of three. Is there a way that we could get closer to the upper end of that range?"

One of two outcomes will arise when asking for more money by consulting these statistics:

1. They have some wiggle room in their budget.
2. You've reached their maximum number.

Let's assume a scenario where the interviewer came out and gave you an initial offer of $72,000.

In most cases, the interviewer will not give you their *maximum* salary number first. If they say "Congratulations, Jim, we're offering you the job. The starting salary is $72,000," do you really think that number is the absolute maximum?

Most likely, they are throwing out a lower number, and *expect* you to counteroffer. However, we've learned that 20 percent of job-seekers *never* counteroffer, so if you don't, that's just more money in their pocket (and not yours).

Photo: Public Domain via Wikipedia

Think of it in the atmosphere of one of America's greatest marketplaces…the yard sale. If someone asks you how much you want for your 1980s Van Halen records and you say, "$40," they'll probably come back and say, "Would you take $20?" You might come back with $30, to which they counteroffer with $25. With all due respect to David Lee Roth, you'll gladly take the twenty-five bucks. Both parties emerge in a win-win scenario because each of you left some wiggle room.

In most cases, the way things unfold if you go through all the steps is that they bump you up a little, you have some more back-and-forth, you eventually settle on a number, and end up in a win-win scenario. If you've managed to play the salary game and not only survive, but thrive, congratulations.

However, the other case is where no matter what you do, no matter what you say, and no matter how convincing your documents are, the number they give is the maximum salary they are willing to pay.

At my first job, the starting salary of every single entry-level tech support representative was $20,000. They wouldn't budge.

During my ESPN interview, I tried counteroffering and listing all the pertinent skills that I was bringing to the job, but they held very firmly to their initial salary offer.

And in many jobs, such as a nonprofit, a school, or the government, there is a fixed rate of compensation that applies to all employees and cannot be changed. Sometimes, it's even public record. For example, did you know that the salary of all rank-and-file members of Congress was $174,000 in 2011?

If you get to the point where they're telling you their maximum, I will also say congratulations. Why?

Remember the questions we wanted to answer:

1. *Was I was prepared?*

2. *Did I do everything I could?*

If you've followed all the steps so far, you were definitely prepared.

If you get to the point where you've negotiated, counteroffered, and reached their maximum offer, you can say that you did everything you could.

At that point, you can honestly sit back and evaluate the job offer for what it is worth. Maybe the salary just isn't what you hoped for, and you decide to decline it. Maybe you're thrilled with the pay and can't wait to start. Or maybe the salary isn't spectacular, but you would be doing something you love and that has great growth potential.

Most important, you stood up for yourself during those ten or fifteen minutes, and you won't be kicking yourself for years saying, "Shoot, I wish I had asked for more money" or "I wonder if they could have gone higher."

Photo: Public Domain via Wikipedia

Step 10: Take 'em for all they're worth

I'm not saying be greedy, but now that you have your optimal salary—or even if you fell a little bit short—don't relax.

Many other perks can be negotiated:

* Title
* Benefits
* Bonuses
* Review periods
* Vacation
* Flextime
* Travel
* Education/seminars

Photo: Jim Hopkinson

A scenario that comes to mind from my life was when I bought a car right after I moved to Seattle. As you can imagine, I did a ton of in-depth research and decided on a used Saab 900, which was safe, fun to drive, and big enough to seat four comfortably for mountain bike trips.

The one thing that made me hesitate was that Saabs weren't at the top of the list in terms of reliability, so to put my mind at ease, I decided to get an extended warranty. I tracked down the perfect car with all the features I wanted, and after an hour of intense negotiation, secured a ridiculous deal on a three-year-old Saab 900S with twenty-one thousand miles.

The salesman then brought me to someone else to talk about the warranty. The slick finance guy turned on the pressure, trying to make the contract seem like a formality by quickly showing me the details and thrusting a pen into my hand. He had definitely done this many times before (maybe he was married to the Evil HR Lady).

Clearly he didn't know whom he was dealing with. I knew that many times a dealer would sacrifice money on the car negotiation, making the buyer feel like he got a great deal by relenting on a $200 sticking point. Then while the customer was basking in the afterglow of the deal, they'd net a $1,000 profit on the warranty. I suspected that was what he was planning here.

In short, the initial warranty he was pushing on me was a horrible deal, and I was able to drastically cut costs by negotiating one that was tailored to my driving habits. I don't think they were happy.

My point is this: It's not that the employer is trying to dupe you and hide additional perks from you; it's that many people focus all of their efforts on salary and neglect to negotiate at all on other items. Ironically, it might be far *easier* for an employer to have flexibility on these items.

In many cases, employee salaries are the largest expense in a company and are tightly monitored. Other benefits like health insurance may also be governed under a strict, company-wide policy. If that's the case, no amount of negotiation is going to get the company to make a special exemption with Aetna just for you.

But sliding you an extra few days of vacation, letting you work from home twice a month, or allocating $1,000 from a separate budget to let you attend that management conference in San Diego in January? Those perks might be easy to pass along, and they'll give you greater peace of mind.

How do you approach these items? With the same tactics I've just taught you.

If your research shows that people with the same seven years of experience at similar companies are called Senior Product Managers instead of Product Managers, ask about it.

If you've read studies that companies are being more flexible with time off and not always sticking to a strict "two weeks' vacation" policy for new employees, ask about it.

If it's really important to you to attend a certain industry trade show or take a class that will help you in your job, ask that it be covered.

Most managers truly want to help out their employees and keep their best workers happy.

Photo: Jim Hopkinson

When you've covered all your bases, remember that it's not always about salary, and you can't put a price on some things:

- The chance to work with a great boss or mentor
- Having good relationships with coworkers
- Achieving a better work–life balance
- Spending less time commuting and more time with family
- Really, really liking what you're doing
- Taking a job that is a stepping stone to, or that *is*, your dream job

Accepting the Job Offer

With everything addressed, you're ready to accept the offer. Remember three things:

- Be thrilled and appreciative.
- Get it in writing.
- Tell them when you will let them know.

When the negotiation is done, the last thing you want is to have your future employer feel like he's given you the world, and then you reply, "Let me think about it." You're coming off a mental battlefield, but it's important that both parties feel like they've won. Therefore, you really want to let them know that you appreciate all their efforts and concessions, and that you'll be worth it.

Still, you want to make sure there's a paper trail so that something negotiated with your future boss doesn't get lost in translation on the way back to payroll. It's also a good idea for you to check over all your notes and make sure that you haven't left something out.

What I recommend is to be very excited, agreeing in theory pending confirmation, and say you just want to sleep on it (or check with a spouse), and promise to get back to them within twenty-four hours. As soon as you can get to a computer, send them a thank you e-mail summarizing the next steps. You might phrase your response as such:

```
Wow, we definitely covered a lot today and I'm really looking forward to
getting down to business. Once I receive your e-mail detailing everything we
spoke about, I'll check over all the details to make sure neither of us missed
anything, and I will get back to you on Friday morning.
```

If your new company doesn't have a dedicated HR department, the burden of navigating all the new-hire details that you just negotiated (salary, bonuses, health plan, vacation time, etc.) might fall to the person you just interviewed with. If they brush away your request to receive a summary of everything you agreed to by saying "Don't worry about it—I think I have everything," that's a signal that you need to take the initiative.

It's almost like when a group of friends and I go out for dinner and we have a waiter who wants to take our entire order from memory, rather than writing it down. It's fine when the first person gets the chicken parmesan and the second person says "I'll have the same," but when Bobby starts ordering sushi, Jayme wants a salad instead of fries, and Phil wants his burger with lettuce and onions but not tomatoes and ketchup, then you know you're in trouble.

Just to be safe, send your new boss an e-mail similar to the one below. Once he sees everything in writing, if there are any discrepancies, they should jump out at him.

Dear Chris,

I am thrilled to accept the position of Senior Designer at Myatt Design at an annual salary of $76,000, beginning on Monday April 5.

From our discussion, the compensation will include:

- Inclusion in the Myatt Design Health/Dental program
- 3 weeks paid vacation per year
- A performance review after six months
- Reimbursement of expenses up to $600 for classes in visual design for mobile applications

Please reply to confirm the above-listed details. I look forward to starting in April.

Sincerely,

Joe Smith

CHAPTER 8
How to Get a Raise in Your Current Job

Without a doubt, the process of pursuing a rewarding new career path, negotiating a great salary, and transitioning into a brand-new job can be life-changing. I'm sure you've been to your share of office going-away parties, where the departing coworker can hardly contain her bubbling excitement as she gushes about the new opportunity, the better title, and the significant increase in pay she's receiving. More than once I've seen these people get taken aside by a less-than-happy cubicle dweller who only half-jokingly whispers "Take me with you. *Please* take me with you."

For people unhappy with their current job or salary level, there is a common assumption: The only way to receive a significant jump in pay is to leave and go to a different company. In many situations, this assumption holds true. As we've seen, most organizations are happy to bump your salary along at a 3–5 percent clip. If you feel you're significantly underpaid or undervalued, the right choice is to change things up and pursue a new opportunity.

But what if you like your current job and just want to earn more money?

What if you're up for an annual salary review and don't want to mess it up?

What if a poor economy has made it difficult to find new opportunities?

In fact, there are many reasons you would choose to stay in your current job. While you might have been thrilled to jump from Chicago to San Francisco to Austin in your twenties to pursue the next big thing, a spouse, three kids, two dogs, and a mortgage can change your perspective in a hurry.

Fortunately, many of the challenges that we covered earlier in the book that are present in a new job search are now an advantage when going for a raise at your current position. For example:

- You don't need to pull off the perfect interview, impress the hiring manager (who you've only known for less than an hour), and convince them why you are the best person among all their candidates for the job; your performance is now being judged by a manager who knows your strengths and, more important, has seen your body of work.
- You don't need to play the cat-and-mouse salary-guessing game to find out how much the position pays; you know exactly what your current compensation is and can negotiate accordingly.
- If you've lived up to your promise as a superstar employee, adding value to the company, generating new business, carving out a niche, and bringing your own mix of personality to the group, you have something of value: leverage. Although you may not *want* to leave, you can still show a quiet confidence that you *could* leave. It is much more difficult, time-consuming, and expensive for your employer to find and train a replacement "to do that thing no one else can do" versus keeping you happy.

However, there's an important distinction between saying "I *received* a raise" and "I *earned* a raise."

In November 2010, Google did something pretty amazing. Not only did it announce that every single one of its 23,000 employees worldwide would receive a 10 percent raise, but they would also get a $1,000 holiday bonus. They even paid the taxes on the bonus so that their workers would receive the full amount!

Have you ever worked for a company where this happened? No? I thought so. Thus, let's consider this the exception.

The far more prevalent scenario is that you have to *earn* your raise. This means you have to work hard, document your successes, know the reasons a company chooses to reward certain employees and not others, and then ask for the raise.

When presenting your case, you must make sure you phrase your argument in terms of how you have helped the company.

Reasons you deserve a raise

- You have made the company money.

- You have saved the company money.
- You do a job no one else can do.

Not reasons you deserve a raise

- They raised your rent./You need more money so that you can afford to move to an apartment in the city. (We *all* have high rent and things are getting more expensive for everyone.)
- The economy is really bad right now. (The economy is bad for everyone, especially businesses.)
- You're getting married/getting divorced/having a baby/buying a house. (Yes, all of these things cost money, but that is not the company's problem.)
- Because Johnny or Suzie just got a raise. (Okay, now you're just whining. But seriously, while you should definitely be paid at a fair value among your peers, you need to prove *your* worth to the company, not someone else's.)

Armed with the negotiation techniques you learned in chapter 6, here are ten steps for getting a raise at your current job.

Step 1: Lay the groundwork

The best negotiations rarely occur when you angrily march into your manager's office, start complaining about how you are underpaid, then demand a raise. A much better idea is to have a plan laid out in advance.

In fact, the first step toward proving your worth as an employee starts on your first day of work. You should maintain a simple list that documents your accomplishments. This doesn't mean you have to constantly have your résumé updated or keep meticulous details about every single project you've worked on. What I do is keep a simple file called accomplishments.txt that I can access quickly to jot down a few bullet points after a major accomplishment on the job. But while the process is simple, the importance is grand—and needs a name as such. Let's call this our...

Accomplishments Manifesto

- Did you just receive a glowing e-mail from a client because you delivered a great project on deadline and under budget? Copy and paste the praise into your document for future reference.

- Did the website you work on have its highest traffic numbers ever due to a marketing program you ran? Note the percentage increase and jot it down.

- Did you bring in new business? Win an award? Learn a new skill needed for the job? It all goes into the Accomplishments Manifesto for safekeeping.

Why? You need to brag a little because you can't always rely on your boss to remember all the things you've done on a day-to-day basis. By creating a quick portfolio of your accomplishments, you can visually document your worth to the company.

Accomplishments Manifesto

- 9/25/10 - Hired as Technical Producer
- 10/20/10 - Secured $30,000 ad buy for Q1 launch
- 11/7/10 - Organized offsite department meeting:
  "I was really impressed with the way you guys pulled off the gig today. From planning it to presenting it to the group, it was well thought out and came off without a hitch."
  – Jim Reiss, VP of Production
- 11/18/10 - Attended focus groups in Chicago with design team to gain customer feedback
- 1/6/11 - Technical project lead for re-launch of entire website, managing a team of 6
- 3/28/11 - Raise / promotion to Senior Technical Producer

Image: Jim Hopkinson / Erin Fitzsimmons

Step 2: Learn the system

Find out in advance how the review system in your company works. Is it handled by the HR department, or does your manager have final say?

In one company I worked for, the process was very formal, involving multipage documents that required me to summarize all of my accomplishments for the past year, and set goals for the following year. Then my manager filled out an equally long evaluation of my strengths, weaknesses, and overall performance. This was followed by a specific meeting to discuss my evaluation, culminating with me signing the form to indicate that I agreed with the direction for the upcoming year. The file was then saved for future reviews.

At other companies, a performance review might be an impromptu meeting where your boss calls you into his office and says "Hey, great job on that last project. We're giving you a bonus. You'll see it in your next paycheck."

Either way, you have to know how the game is played before you can score some points.

Step 3: Decide on timing

While you can certainly ask for a raise any day of the year, it's in your best interest to know what the overall budget cycle is for your business.

Most businesses run on a fiscal calendar (not necessarily January through December), so you will want to find out when budgets are being developed and time your inquiry for a salary increase at the proper moment. You don't want to sit down and ask for a raise, only to be told, "Oh, I'm so sorry, you should have talked to me two weeks ago. We've just locked down the budget and I won't have any money allocated for raises until the next fiscal year."

The other thing to consider is when reviews are done.

In some cases, evaluations will follow the budget cycle above, and all employees are judged for raises or bonuses at the same time.

At other companies, employees are reviewed based on their individual hire dates.

Step 4: Get noticed and increase communication

Although you'll be armed with a laundry list of successes from your previous projects via your Accomplishments Manifesto, managers do suffer a little from "What have you done for me lately?" syndrome. Therefore, as you're preparing to ask for a raise or your annual salary review approaches, focus on high-profile projects that have more visibility within the company.

If you're in sales, of course you want to keep all your current accounts happy. But if that review is approaching, consider spending some extra time trying to lure that big account that the company has always wanted to land.

If you're with a more traditional company that's making a new push online, volunteer to help with the launch of the new website.

If your company hosts a special event or conference, this is a great way to gain visibility. No matter how well the agenda is planned, there can never be enough people on hand to help handle the last-minute crisis that is sure to pop up. Get there early, stay late, and make sure the attendees have an amazing experience.

In other words, involvement with just about anything that will raise your profile is a good idea.

Let me give you a real-world example.

Someone I know (we'll call him Joseph) works at a large company, and the management team decided to create an internal contest, with the goal of engaging employees, fostering new ideas, and helping develop their long-term strategy. Let's call it "the Big Idea."

All that was required was that one or more employees come up with a new and innovative idea that the company could potentially use, then put together a fifteen-minute presentation to senior management. They had to describe what the idea was, how it would be executed, the costs involved, and the revenue model.

Joseph had worked at the company for several years and was fairly well known. While he read the entire e-mail about the contest when it came into his inbox and a few thoughts came to mind, he filed it away as "just another corporate program." But then Ann, a younger coworker Joseph knew well and who had only been with the company a month, came bounding up to his desk.

"Did you see that e-mail? I think we should enter the contest! I have a few ideas I want to brainstorm with you over lunch." Joseph was intrigued and inspired by her energy, and by the end of lunch they had sketched out a plan:

- The idea would revolve tightly around the company's brand, one of its greatest strengths.
- To be innovative and looking toward the future, they would design a product for the Apple iPad, which had just been released six months prior.
- Joseph, an experienced public speaker, would design and deliver the presentation.
- Ann, a design and technical whiz, would create something they were pretty sure no one else would have: an actual demo on the iPad that could be passed around.

All in all, they spent only an hour or two for a few nights after work putting together the presentation. Out of the hundreds and hundreds of employees given the chance to have their voices heard in front of the highest level of decision makers in the company, can you guess how many teams presented?

About a dozen.

Was the end result a failure because they were narrowly edged out by another team and didn't win the Big Idea contest? Not by a long shot.

- Joseph was able to reassert his value to the company in front of the highest levels of management as a leader, an innovator, and an entertaining public speaker.
- Ann was able to put herself on the map, getting off on the right foot with her new boss and being recognized as an up-and-comer within the company.
- The idea was so well received that they were asked to give the presentation again to the president of the company, who had been unable to attend their session.
- Ann bonded with one of the senior executives in the room, went to coffee with her the next week, and is now using her as a mentor.

Joseph put it to me this way: "I only invested about five hours of time, and what I got back was a really valuable bullet point." What did he mean by that?

- When it's time to update his résumé, he has a new bullet point that says, "Runner-up in companywide innovation contest presented to senior management."

- When he's asked on an interview, "Tell me about a time when you showed initiative," he has a great answer.
- And when he sits down with his manager later that month for his performance review, he has the ammunition he needs to prove that he is a successful leader, communicator, and forward-thinking employee providing value to the company, which will help him justify his request for a raise.

As I just showed, becoming more involved in the company is a great way to raise your profile. But it's not going to help much if your boss doesn't know about it, so you may need to increase your communication with her.

As your performance review or raise discussion nears, go a little "cc:" happy.

This doesn't mean you should spam your manager or constantly brag about the projects you're involved with, but like your Accomplishments Manifesto, you want to keep your boss (and in select cases, your boss's boss) in the loop on things.

Forward them the latest version of the project you're working on, include them on the invite to the presentations you're doing, and make sure they know when milestones are reached.

Doing so may invoke what is known in psychology as the recency effect. This refers to a person's tendency to recall a disproportionate amount of recent observations and events.

So if you're up for a review at the end of the year, if you remind him enough about the successful project in October, the 10 percent bump in sales in November, and how you covered for your department during the holiday break, your boss might just forget that you lost a big client in the spring and took a three-week vacation over the summer.

Message	Insert	Options	Format Text

To... Rob Thompson; Krish Gupta; Suzanne Parks
Cc... Tom Nicholas; Elizabeth Wideman
Bcc...
Subject: Website re-launch timelines
Attached: Relaunch-Project-Plan.xls (17 KB)

Hi team

We are on track to meet our launch date of January 6 and the client is extremely happy with their sponsorship.

Attached is the latest project plan.

- Joe

Joseph DeStefan
Technical Project Leader
212-555-1212

Image: Jim Hopkinson/Erin Fitzsimmons

93

Step 5: Set a date

When asking for a raise, you don't want to catch your boss off guard. Mention casually that you're going over your goals for the next six months, and that you'd like to discuss your next steps at the company.

Then, send an official invite and set up an appointment one to two weeks in the future to get on your boss's calendar. Be smart about the day and time that you choose. As you're working, notice which days of the week are most hectic for your boss or filled with the most meetings, and avoid those. Most e-mail programs, such as Microsoft Outlook, allow you to view your boss's calendar and see what times are available.

Does your boss get in early and start the day with a huge cup of coffee? Make an early-morning appointment.

Is your boss immediately swamped with meetings and e-mails in the morning? If so, a time later in the day might be best. If possible, plan your meeting so that it doesn't bump up against other meetings that she needs to prepare for.

Setting a date a week or two out gives your boss time to reschedule if there is an important project going on or if a vacation is planned. Then, send a quick e-mail the day before to confirm that you're still on and remind her of your discussion.

Step 6: Know their style

When presenting to your boss the reasons you deserve a raise or promotion, it's important to know his or her style. If your boss is a no-nonsense, bottom-line type of manager, make sure you keep the information to a minimum, but provide him or her with lots of numbers and hard facts that prove your worth.

If your boss is a more social, nurturing type of manager, use your data to paint a picture and tell a story of your involvement with the group and how you're helping the company as a whole succeed.

As a general rule, the higher your boss is up the corporate ladder, from manager to director to vice president to owner, the more likely it is that he or she focuses on "big picture" data. To be clear, you should be intimately familiar with every detail from your Accomplishments Manifesto. If asked about the bottom-line numbers of a particular project, you should be able to provide them from memory or have supporting documents with you.

However, the key here is to communicate the highlights of your accomplishments, your value to the company, your goals for the future, and what you're asking for in return.

© iStockphoto.com/Neustockimages

© iStockphoto.com/ZoneCreative

Step 7: Know your options

What if things don't go as planned? Should you threaten to leave the company and say you have another offer (even if you don't)?

Giving your supervisor an ultimatum and saying "If I don't get a raise, I'm leaving" is definitely a high-risk tactic, but it does give you a lot of leverage. Employees are expensive commodities within a company to find, hire, train, and retain, and in most cases it's a lot easier to give you a few thousand dollars more or a higher title versus finding someone else.

However, if you use this tactic, you must be prepared to walk. In the end, do you really want a bidding war? For example, let's say you've been at your company for five years and are making $50,000 per year, but you haven't received a raise in the last two years. You go on another interview and they offer you $56,000.

You tell your boss, she says she doesn't want you to leave, and she counteroffers for $60,000.

You're faced with an interesting situation. If you were excited about the potential new job, you now have to go back to them and either decline their offer or ask for more money (which they might not be able to provide).

If you stay with your current job, now you might be asking, "Why did it take them so long to pay me what I'm worth, and they only did so when I threatened to leave?" And if you do decide to stay, now your boss knows that you weren't completely happy before and were interviewing behind her back.

Of course, if you're completely happy with either option, and the end result is that you get more money and are paid what you're worth, then you have two great outcomes. Just be sure you play out all possible scenarios beforehand.

In the end, it's all about knowing your options, your value in the marketplace, and having a little bit of leverage. One salesperson I used to work with told me that he goes on at least one interview every six months, even if he's happy in his current job. In doing so, he makes sure he knows his current worth, finds out what skills are most valuable in his constantly changing field, and has potential "escape routes" should something come up at his current job.

Step 8: Having the right mind-set

Okay, the day has come. You walk into your boss's office, you sit down, and after exchanging pleasantries about the weather or the upcoming weekend (complimenting the photo of his cute puppy can't hurt, either), your boss says, "So what's on your mind?"

Once again, it's time to utilize the Master Mind-set. You are not begging for a raise. You aren't demanding that you be recognized. And you're not hoping that they please please please give you more money.

In many ways, this is a *business* transaction. You have to honestly feel in your mind—and prove via supporting arguments—that you have worked very hard to provide added value to the company, and the company should compensate you for what you've contributed. It's a two-way street.

Step 9: Make your case

By now you should know what you're going to say and have practiced how you're going to say it. Your presentation should take into account the personality of your boss (Step 6) but also *your* personality.

Here are three ways your presentation might go...

1. Off the cuff

If you're a no-nonsense person comfortable with a free-flowing conversation, then simply have a few bullet points in mind and let it fly. This might work better with a supervisor who also has the same type of personality.

An example might be a salesperson asking the Vice President of Sales for a raise. I asked Robert Shanes, who runs his own company and has been in sales for twenty years, "What is the best possible way that a salesperson could come to you asking for a raise?" Here's how he tells it:

> When someone comes to me looking for a raise, of course I care that they're a good employee, that the customers are happy, that they do all their paperwork correctly, and a host of other small things.
>
> But in terms of evaluating a salesperson in a performance review, if I break it down to the most basic elements, it would be based around two things:
>
> 1. Effort
> 2. Results
>
> The only real way to gauge whether or not they are going to get to the latter is how they are approaching the former. Furthermore, effort can also be broken down into the type of sales calls they make, as judged by two factors:
>
> 1. Quality
> 2. Quantity

Looking at these elements—and the numbers produced from them—the perfect pitch would be something like this:

Hi, Robert. Thanks for taking the time to sit down with me today. In our annual sales meeting, you addressed the team about achieving higher *quality* visits with clients, and efficiently increasing the *quantity* of visits. Here is how I've done that:

Increasing quality

- I began with stronger preparation. I am now walking into my meetings with more customized presentations and competitive analysis than ever before, and the clients have noticed.
- Next, I focused on ensuring that my meetings have multiple people in attendance. There has consistently been 25% more people at each visit, and I've been able to follow up with each of them effectively.
- Finally, as you suggested, I've been taking more detailed notes in each meeting so that I was sure to have my action items spelled out before leaving. This has enabled us to reduce the turnaround time required to get a quote back to the client from 4–5 days to 2.

Increasing quantity

- In order to increase the number of meetings I was having, I knew I had to expand into new markets. I was able to step up efforts with the government and hospital verticals, signing five new clients between the two of them, including the Sunrise Square deal for $140k.
- You also introduced the idea of more efficient travel. I managed to increase the number of meetings I had each month by 17% by better grouping geographically, using our database program efficiently, and getting assistance from our local dealer network, yet my expenses remained constant.

Summary

- Because I was able to step up my efforts in increasing both the quality and quantity of meetings, my sales increased nearly 20% last year and almost 30% in the last quarter alone. I feel that I've grown my territory consistently while keeping a keen eye on expenses and efficient use of travel. I look forward to having another stellar year, am hopeful that the company sees the value I bring, and would like to discuss an increase in my compensation to reflect these efforts.

"If a salesperson delivered a pitch like that," Shanes summed up, "clearly articulating his value to the company, showing that he was aligned with our goals, having data to support his cause, and not complaining about difficult clients or making excuses, I would definitely give him a raise."

2. Supporting documentation

Whereas the salesperson's mantra can be whittled down to a single word (*Sell!*), many people have a job covering a multitude of responsibilities. In this case, you'll want to highlight several of your accomplishments and bring supporting data for your supervisor to see.

A close friend of mine, Matt Tracy, is an executive chef at one of the leading private clubs in the United States. The range and scope of his job would make most people's head spin. Which is why, when he goes in to speak to the club manager regarding his compensation, he's incredibly prepared.

As always, information is your best friend.

The format he uses is to consolidate everything he wants to highlight onto a bulleted list on a single sheet of paper, much like a résumé. He then brings additional supporting documents to back that up if the manager wants to drill deeper on a certain point. The layout might look like this (actual numbers have been changed):

Budget

- Club memberships sold increased 10 percent this year from 2,500 to 2,750, leading to $1.25 million in additional revenue.

- Food and Beverage costs were reduced by $40,000, meeting our goal.
- We served 183,500 meals.
- The club had food sales of $2.5M, exceeding our budget goal by 6 percent despite a down economy.
- Supporting document: Budget

Club Member Satisfaction

- Member satisfaction reached an all-time high, with an 88 percent favorable rating based on our recent survey.
- The dining experience remains the largest perceived benefit according to club members, and strong word of mouth helps existing members recommend it to their friends.
- This year we changed menus much more often, updating our offerings several times per week to keep current with food that is regional and seasonal.
- Sample feedback: "I've really noticed an increase in quality of the meals, especially the weekend brunch. Hats off to Chef Tracy and the rest of the kitchen staff."
- Supporting document: Recent survey highlights and sample menus

New Events

- In addition to our traditional "tent pole" events such as Easter, Mother's Day, Thanksgiving, and New Years, we added seven significant new events this year. Our three most successful were:
  - Tri-city Triathlon lunch. More than 125 members watched the conclusion of the race a few blocks from the club, then came in for lunch, driving $25,000 in revenue.
  - Fourth of July Clambake. This event was wildly successful, attracting 243 members and also raising $3,000 for charity.

- Wednesday night Jazz. Attendance on Wednesdays—the slowest night of the week—was up 17 percent, while providing members with a new experience.
- Supporting documents: Marketing advertisements for each event

Management and Leadership

- As a ServSafe certified trainer, I've made sure each employee has successfully passed the required training.
- We have promoted three staff members to full-time, expanded our list of part-time contract workers for peak rush hour, while cutting payroll costs 5 percent.
- The morale of the kitchen staff is much improved versus last year, and the entire team is functioning as a cohesive unit.

Notice the four key points that Matt focuses on.

First, he went right to the bottom line. He knows the general manager is a no-nonsense guy, under pressure from the board of directors to meet his numbers, so he wanted to give him the financials first.

Second, he talks about the club members and their dining experience. Without paying members at the club, neither of them would have a job. The club does continual satisfaction surveys, and he knows that the high score they received this year is a huge source of pride.

Next, he focuses on new business. This goes hand in hand with the last point, as the club wants to be innovative with new and exciting events so members will see value for their membership.

Finally, he talks about the staff. If you've ever worked in the restaurant business, you know that the job is incredibly demanding, with a high degree of turnover. Employees are on their feet for as much as twelve hours at a time, often, as the saying goes, "slaving in front of a hot stove."

I remember a business management class I once took in college. The professor asked us how we could motivate employees. My mind instantly pictured a sprawling office tower filled with men and women wearing suits and sitting in front of computers. Ideas that were given included increased salary, cash bonuses, travel perks, casual Fridays, flextime, and stock option plans.

But then the professor threw us a curveball: How would you motivate a dishwasher?

The level of job prevents you from handing out lavish salaries, bonuses, and stock options. Their choice of clothing comes down to wearing something they don't mind getting dirty. And there is no telecommuting option or travel perks…when the dishes pile up, they need to be washed. Now.

I'm not sure anyone in the class ever came up with a great answer that day, so I asked Matt, a twenty-year veteran with the unique ability to make everyone on his staff feel like an integral part of the team.

He replied, "I start every single day on the job the same way, by going around and shaking the hand of each and every employee that works for me. I look them in the eye and say hello. It doesn't matter if they are a sous chef, a waiter, a busboy, or a dishwasher; I let them know that they are all equally valued. Then at the end of the day, I do the same thing, thanking them for their work."

So although Matt began his performance review with numbers, he ended it with that story.

He told the general manager, "Remember a few weeks ago when we grabbed a drink after work, and you came by and asked if I was ready, and I said, 'Not yet'? It was because I needed to shake everyone's hand."

The GM paused and said, "Do you really need to do that *every* day?"

Matt replied, "Yes, I do. Last month I was running late and missed one of the dishwashers on the way out. The next morning, as I was sitting in my office, I heard a quiet knock on the door. I looked up and the dishwasher was standing there, shifting nervously back and forth on his feet, and looking rather sheepish. I asked what was wrong, and he said, 'Chef Tracy, are you upset with me? You didn't shake my hand last night.' Even though I assured him that everything was okay, I felt horrible."

The moral here? While it is vitally important to back up your accomplishments with hard data, there are intangible traits like the ability to lead a team that can be measured only with words and actions. If you can illustrate that, it makes it easy for a manager to justify a pay increase.

3. The Digital Portfolio

Let me say it again: Know your audience. If the salesperson with the gift of gab or the executive chef running a bustling kitchen were to pitch their boss using an interactive portfolio on the iPad, they'd probably be told, "Put that stupid computer away and tell me what you want." Best to leave the digital portfolios to designers, right?

Not necessarily.

Once purely the realm of designers and photographers, having a personal portfolio of your work has expanded to other categories. As a marketer, I have a portfolio that I've brought to interviews for a few years now. I chose a professional-looking art portfolio "display book" from a company called Itoya (http://www.itoya.com). They come in various sizes and run about $10–$20. I used the 9" × 12" size, which allowed me to easily insert standard 8½" × 11" printouts and documents, while giving a little breathing room and having a nice border around it.

There are a few advantages of a portfolio:

1. It's a powerful visual demonstration. As the saying goes, a picture is worth a thousand words. If every job candidate is *telling* the hiring manager what she did in her last job, but you're physically *showing* him, it carries so much more weight.

2. It shifts the control of the interview back to you. If the interviewer is firing questions at you and you're not doing as well as you could fielding them, reply to them by asking permission to show them an example.

    So, for instance, they say, "Tell me about a time you led a successful group project." You reply, "I had a very interesting project at my last job hosting an off-site event for our new product launch. Would you mind if I showed you a few examples from it in my portfolio?"

    You can then jump to the pages that show event invitations, marketing materials, photos, etc.

3. It allows you to tell a story. My portfolio is strategically laid out to cover various skills that I possess, building from strategy (marketing plans, creative briefs) to marketing materials (websites, banners, e-mails, and newsletters) to business expertise (budgets, reporting, analytics, results) to, finally, a page or two with some fun human-interest elements.

But just as photos from film cameras, videos on VHS tapes, and music on records and cassettes have all gone digital, so has the portfolio. In retrospect, it was interesting that as a digital marketing manager, I was presenting so many of my online projects in paper form. Of course, I could have displayed my work on a laptop, but lugging around a heavy computer, booting up, and clearing room to plop down a fifteen-inch machine on your interviewer's desk could be quite awkward.

But now two things have changed.

1) JUST ABOUT ANYONE CAN USE A DIGITAL PORTFOLIO

If you're reading this book—and certainly if you're reading it as an e-book—the chances are pretty high that you sit at a computer for a large majority of your day and are familiar with technology.

Even if you're not a website designer or digital marketer, you are probably familiar with PowerPoint, Excel, web research, social media, and blogs. I'm willing to bet you also own a camera that takes digital photos and videos.

So no matter what your job, you have the tools to illustrate the things you do on a day-to-day basis in digital form.

- Accountant? Take screenshots of your balanced budget and year-end graphs from Excel.
- Director at a nonprofit? Take photos of the impoverished country you visited when setting up their support program.
- Assistant event planner? Shoot a quick video of the recent concert or conference you helped organize.

2) SMALL, PERSONAL, TABLET COMPUTERS ARE THE NEW PORTFOLIO

On January 7, 2010, amid much fanfare, rumors, and hype, Apple announced the iPad. It was an immediate success, selling 3 million units in the first eighty days following its release on April 3, and at the time becoming the fastest selling electronic device ever. It went on to sell nearly 15 million units in 2010 alone.

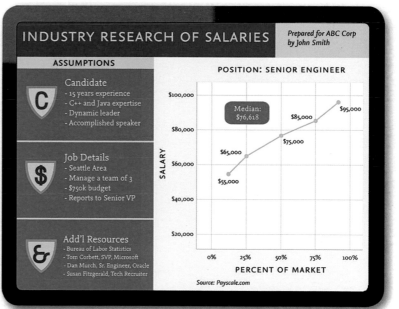

Tablet photo: © iStockphoto.com/alexsl
IRS image: Erin Fitzsimmons/JimHopkinson

In short, the iPad—and the multitude of tablets released in its wake—is a fantastic way to display the projects you've worked on. Not only can you walk your current or prospective employer through your accomplishments, but you can also display your IRS document when you get to salary talk.

(Go to SalaryTutor.com for examples of digital portfolios.)

The goal with the digital portfolio?

If you're going for a raise in your current job, it's a quick, visual, compelling way for your supervisor to swipe through your accomplishments of the past year. While a great portfolio won't necessarily get you a raise if you don't have the work history to back it up, it certainly shows initiative and is a great jumping-off point for discussion.

If you're going for a new position, there are two words I'll leave you with:

Be Memorable.

Until the day when every job searcher is walking into an interview with a professional-looking portfolio to highlight their work, bringing something unique to the table might just give you an edge in a competitive environment.

Want the ultimate proof? Major League Baseball outfielder Carl Crawford made the news after the 2010 season when his agent sent iPads stocked with a preloaded highlight reel and testimonials to teams interested in signing his client.

The result? Crawford later signed a seven-year, $142 million contract with the Boston Red Sox. Am I suggesting that a digital portfolio could also help *you* land a nine-figure payday? Um, not exactly. The highly coveted free agent was going to make millions no matter what happened, and his body of work, including every possible statistic and hundreds of hours of video, were easily available for all to see. But you have to admit, it *was* memorable.

In short, if you focus on your value to the company and the hard facts that show your contributions, a smart company will do the right thing and keep their best employees happy.

Step 10: Keep your cool

Once you've effectively laid out your case to your boss, have a plan for how you'll handle their response.

Some managers will be willing to work out the details on the spot, so you'll need to fall back on the negotiating skills covered earlier in the book. Be ready with a range that you're willing to accept, practice the "Right Back at Ya" Method and silent response, and ask for some time to think over their offer if needed.

In other cases, you might not get an immediate answer. Although you should have put in a few hours of preparation for this moment, even if this was a scheduled annual review, your supervisor may need to work out the numbers with Human Resources, verify the budget with company owners, or determine the level of raises for your entire department before offering a final number.

While you should never issue an ultimatum for an answer, definitely pressure your supervisor for a date when this can be settled. Then, head back to your desk, send an e-mail thanking him for the meeting, and set a reminder for the follow-up discussion.

What if you don't like the response? Less than desirable outcomes could be your company offering a much lower raise than you anticipated, denying the raise due to business conditions or budget concerns, or outright honesty in telling you that you don't deserve a raise.

No matter the outcome, keep your cool in the meeting. Throwing a tantrum won't make things better, now or down the line. After you've made your pitch, it's time to truly listen to what your company is telling you.

If the company is doing poorly enough that they can't properly reward top performers, it might make sense to take whatever is offered and start shopping your résumé.

If your boss seems genuine, and truly would like to give you a raise but can't, ask questions to dig deeper and find out ways that you can work together to reach a mutually beneficial outcome.

If the response is that your work has not been up to par and you are not worthy of that promotion you've been banking on, it might be just the reality check you need. As difficult as it may be, take some time for self-reflection and ask yourself if you are truly performing at your highest level.

Perhaps your skills are outdated, and this is an opportunity for additional training. Maybe you've become too content at your job and have just been coasting by on past performance. When you really examine things, you might even conclude that the work you're doing just isn't fulfilling to you anymore, and this could serve as a wake-up call to explore another career that you are more passionate about.

Negotiating salary in a bad economy

When the stock market is booming, housing values are skyrocketing, and sales are coming in from all angles, it's a little easier to ask for a piece of the pie. But when the forecast is doom and gloom, does that mean you should completely write off the chances of getting a raise? Not quite.

Know the situation

Similar to knowing the budget calendar, you need to know your company's health. Nothing will get you an instant no faster than walking in and asking for a 15 percent raise if a dozen people were just laid off and there's been a hiring freeze for the past three months. A humorous line going around during the worst of the recession in 2010 was "Not getting laid off is the new getting promoted." So know your place.

It's all about the money

During the good times, there's more room for companies to develop branding, gain market share, and explore new markets. But when things get lean, it's all about cash flow. In almost all cases, anything that is going to bring in direct revenue will be prioritized highest, so put yourself in a position to work on these revenue-generating projects.

Depending on your position and the company, opportunities to "trade cash flow for cash" may exist. What does that mean? While you might not be able to get a straight raise, incentives for bringing in new business might be rewarded. For example, propose to your manager a situation where, if you meet X goal and bring in Y amount of business, you'll get a percentage of that. It becomes win-win because they don't have to pay you if you don't perform, but both of you look good if money is coming into the company.

Set the stage for the recovery

In a bad economy, it's still okay to ask for a meeting with your boss to talk about your career objectives. Sit down and make it clear that you understand the current climate. Say that you know that it's difficult to give raises now, but show that you *deserve* one based on your work.

This could be the best time to ask for a higher *title*. If you've proven your worth, your boss might feel bad that they can't reward you monetarily but will happily bump you from, say, manager to senior manager. Then ask for a review in six months, whether the economy rebounds or not, and put it on the calendar.

What you've done is set the stage for recovery. If the economy does rebound in six months, press them for the salary increase that would have gone along with your recent bump in title. If you're still seeing resistance within your company, at least when you start shopping your résumé around, you've got a higher title to command more money at your next opportunity.

What it says about you

Sure, your coworkers might think you're crazy for setting up these meetings when institutions around you are going belly-up, and your boss might incredulously ask, "You're asking for a raise in *this* economy? You're lucky you still have a job!"

However, a good supervisor knows your forward-thinking planning says something unique about you. Just the fact that you are *aware* of the situation, are communicating openly with your boss about your career objectives, and are tracking your accomplishments shows initiative and focus.

It also helps you understand the business when you realize the areas that are most critical to survival when times are lean. And rather than burying your head like other employees, you're trying to focus on the positive and build for the future.

Most important, speaking up will keep you on your boss's radar, and it lets her know you're looking to advance. Think about it…when the business *does* start to roar back to life, who is the first person she'll have in mind when it's time for reviews?

Negotiation for Freelancers 9

At this point, I've walked you through negotiation techniques when going for a new job and dealing with a potential boss, and how to get a raise at your current position from your existing boss.

But what if you're your own boss?

Freelancers and small business owners face different challenges than standard full-time employees. Working for a large corporation may provide a formalized review process, annual raise opportunities, and a clear path to be promoted up through the ranks. For those craving structure, it's an ideal situation that lets you set goals for the year, prove your worth to your employer, and justify pay and title increases accordingly.

While there is no such structure for the freelancer, there are many benefits of being your own boss. In addition to the freedom it provides—choosing how to run your business, where you want to work, who you want to work with, and what hours you want to keep—a great advantage is that you are in control of how much you charge customers, and thus how much you earn.

Take the example of a freelance graphic designer charging $50 per hour in January. If customers are happy, business picks up, and the market will bear it, they can begin charging $60 or $70 per hour for new clients in March. Quite the difference versus waiting for an annual performance review a year later.

In fact, for a small business owner dealing with multiple clients, every single day could bring a new negotiation. Get good at it, and the sky's the limit for how successful you can be.

But life as a freelancer is not all working from home in your jammies and going on vacation whenever you want. It comes with a long list of unique challenges.

Fortunately, we've built an excellent foundation of negotiation techniques. If you're a freelancer and jumped directly to this section, go back and at least review chapter 6. There are many skills we covered that will be useful in any negotiation:

- Doing competitive research
- Building a strong network
- Preparing supporting documentation
- Prompting the other party to answer the compensation question first
- Finding out their range with the "Right Back at Ya" Method
- Using FBI negotiation techniques to arrive at the highest dollar figure

Once you have those skills mastered, you can move on to my negotiation tips for freelancers. Because I have worked mostly full-time in my career, I reached out to my network of successful freelance friends for advice, from Boston to Brooklyn and SoHo to Seattle.

What I got back was not necessarily a blueprint for the "thirty seconds to glory" confrontation that occurs between interviewer and interviewee at the key moment when salary is discussed, but rather a set of fundamental rules that freelancers should live by in order to have the greatest success in terms of compensation. Thus I give you...

10 freelance fundamentals

1. Truly believe in the value of your service

When you receive a huge invoice from the surgeon who removed your appendix or the mechanic who replaced your car's transmission, it's difficult to argue with their expertise because there's probably very little chance you could have performed that process yourself.

But in an age where 12-megapixel cameras are under $100 and free blogging software abounds, it can be difficult to convince some people to pay a premium for a photographer or web designer.

The first thing you need to do is adapt the Master Mind-set and truly believe that what you do adds value, and have the confidence to back it up. In March 2010 I interviewed Diana Levine (http://www.dianalevine.com), a New York–based freelance photographer who has built up her freelance career to the point where she shoots professional celebrities such as Kim Kardashian, 50 Cent, Ludacris, Alicia Keys, and Elvis Costello. (She also is the photographer who did my author photo.)

I asked her what she would say to people who were thinking about doing the photography themselves at an event rather than hire a professional who does it for a living. Her answer was very interesting:

> I think it drives some photographers nuts that everyone can get a DSLR and be a photographer. But actually, I love it. I love that everyone can get a camera. I think that everyone should have a camera. I think that everyone should be a photographer.
>
> The only thing it changes is that you have to be even better; you have to really make yourself different. You have to be special enough that someone's going to hire you as opposed to getting their friend to do it.
>
> In addition, I would say a big part of using a professional photographer, in the instance that you're shooting a celebrity, is that there's no room for error such as having your camera or lighting break down. So a big part of being a professional is knowing how to handle certain situations, being prepared with backup equipment, and knowing how to roll with the punches.

So if your brother-in-law offers to shoot your wedding photos with his new DSLR, think twice about how he'll handle bright sunshine casting dark shadows outside the church, fluorescent lights indoors at the reception, and a dead battery with no backup.

© iStockphoto.com/chaoss

The next thing you need to do is compare yourself to the competition and arm yourself with data.

Meghan O'Neill, a New York–based Web and Interactive Media Designer, referred me to the Creative Group (http://www.creativegroup.com), which each year publishes a comprehensive salary guide that "provides starting salaries for more than 100 creative, interactive, marketing, and public relations positions. It also includes information on current hiring trends and a formula for localizing salary levels for major markets."

By keeping abreast of what the rest of the industry is charging, you can price your work accordingly.

2. Consider the full scope of any project

I cautioned that when looking at a traditional job, salary should be only one of many factors to consider, along with health benefits, vacation, commute time, work/life balance, and the long-term prospects for your career.

The same is true with freelancers. Negotiating a fair price is key, but it is also important to consider the full scope of a project and how it will impact your business in both the short and long term.

Erin Fitzsimmons (http://www.efitzdesign.com), the Brooklyn-based designer who did all the original design work for *Salary Tutor*, said the following:

> There's more to the negotiation package than just the monetary fee. Often, if I can tell that a client has a strong web presence and will give me free promotion as part of the deal, I'm willing to accept a lower amount.
>
> I had one client who offered me a very low fee, but with the prospect of future work designing their logo and business identity. For the logo project, I was able to charge by the hour; thus, in the end, I was paid an adequate fee for the sum of work provided.
>
> In this case, the client did have issues understanding why a logo design cost more

than an entire book layout, and I had to respectfully remind them that I accepted the lower fee for the book only because I expected additional fees for the logo.

This client has since promoted me on Twitter and on their website, and has provided personal recommendations to other authors seeking a book designer. It's definitely a balancing act.

Another close friend—let's call her Maya—is a former Design Director at a major apparel company, and is now the owner and cofounder of her own design firm. When considering whether to take on a new project, here is how she looks at the big picture:

Photo: Jim Hopkinson

Some types of projects are easy, creative, zen, and flow easily. Other projects are trouble at every turn. We charge less for some types of work that we really enjoy. We always try to be flexible on pricing. If the project is good for your growth, inspiring, new, or innovative, you may have to give a little on your pricing.

A little start-up is one of my favorite clients. They can't pay as much as the big companies, but we work very, very well together:

- Communication is very casual.
- Their deadlines are flexible.
- They require very few in-office meetings.
- They are very reliable repeat business.

Because of the lack of aggravation, it is worth the reduced rate, and I don't even mind working nights or weekends on their projects if needed.

The type of work you take on may also be tied directly to the stage your freelance business is in.

Helen Todd is cofounder of Sociality Squared, a social media consulting firm based in New York City. She also manages a Facebook marketing blog (http://www.fbadz.com). Let's hear how she got her business off the ground:

When I first started my business, it was so important to take on clients that I was willing to undervalue my services just to get my foot in the door. It was a calculated risk that took into consideration how the client would build my résumé, if it would turn into a long-term business relationship, and if I would still be able to cover my bills.

I also knew that as a brand-new company, despite my extensive experience, I still couldn't charge the higher end of the industry until I had built some credibility on my own. I was very fortunate to land a client with international brand recognition in the luxury market four months after opening up shop.

This particular client wanted to experiment with social media, and the budget allocated for it wasn't too high, but since they were willing to work with a brand-new company and sign on for six months, it made sense for me to work with them.

We worked on a contract and outlined exactly what my company's services would include. Over those six months, there were definitely times that this client realized our talent and added more responsibilities to my plate.

There were also times when I knew that I was going far above and beyond the terms of the contract, but I was okay with that. Not only was I building great case studies, but also social media was becoming more and more important to the company as my services helped them realize the power of the social web."

We'll see how this eventually turned out for Helen's business in Step 9.

3. Find the right projects

Now that you know to look at the big picture when considering a project, how do you decide on the right one? The type of client you work with will dramatically affect how much you can charge and the amount of negotiation leverage you have.

Marina Fish is a freelance designer and owner of Marina Fish Design (http://www.marinafish.com) in Seattle. How does she choose the right projects?

This took a long time to figure out. Charging a higher rate changes whom you work for. For example, someone working as a VP of Marketing has a marketing budget. They are spending someone else's money, and it is assumed there will be X number of dollars spent for design, copywriting, engineering, etc. They are happy to pay a professional rate, or keep someone on retainer for a certain number of hours per month. They also usually have someone else helping with all the other parts of a project (messaging, e-mail campaign, trade show elements, etc).

This is different from a small business owner who may not be tech savvy but wants a new or updated brand and is paying with their own money. Someone at this level also generally wants web development, copywriting, and a marketing plan along with design. These types of clients have shown discomfort at my rate, and I have to attribute it to lack of knowledge about what designers do, so I find I need to provide a higher level of education about all the elements involved.

Is there really a difference between working with companies versus individuals when negotiating a rate?

Yes, said Twanna Hines, a Manhattan-based relationships writer (http://www.funkybrownchick.com):

When you're negotiating with a company, generally there is a budget, so at least there's a target range. Before I give an exact quote, I find out what that range is, and then you are just dealing with whether you're on the low end or the high end of that range.

But many times in freelance, *you* are the person who is establishing that range, and it could vary widely depending on both parties. So the key is to know your worth and stick to it, even if it turns out that the two parties are far off and not a good fit for each other. You can't be afraid to turn down a client because you can't settle on a number.

Helen Todd echoed that sentiment:

Knowing when to say no to a client that isn't a good fit can be just as important as saying yes to one that is. Depending on where you are in your business, it's very hard to hold your ground, especially if some cash will help keep you afloat.

But remember this: If you take on that new, ill-advised client just for the cash, you're taking away time to work on a longer-standing client, as well as time spent bringing in new business that will help you grow as a brand.

4. Don't quote a price during the first meeting

When you're running your own business, it means you're always out there "hustling." It doesn't matter if you're at a conference for your industry, at your Uncle Sherman's fiftieth birthday party, or waiting with other mommies to pick up your child at daycare, you never know when someone new will ask, "So, what do you do for a living?"

First of all, the easiest and most obvious thing to do—and yet I'm still astonished at the number of people I meet who don't have this—is to have a business card. The reason some people might not have them is that business cards cost about $400 and take months to design and create.

Oh wait, my bad. On a site like OvernightPrints.com, you can get cards for about $4 and have them shipped to you overnight if you wish, and on Vistaprint.com you can actually get cards made up using one of their dozens of templates for *free*. So seriously, get some business cards, make sure your phone number and e-mail address are on there, and direct them to your website so they can see some samples of your work.

So what happens when the mother of Aiden (or was it Caden? or maybe Jayden?) comes up to you and asks you to design a simple website for her new Mommy-Blog idea? While it's tempting to hear her out and try to quote a price off the top of your head, it's a much better plan to take it all in, give her a business card, and then get back to her with a price.

This allows you to fully plan out the amount of work on the project, make sure it's a good fit for your business, and perhaps exchange a few e-mails to make sure you're both on the same page in terms of scope.

One of the red flags for some designers is if the first question out of the mouth of a potential client is "How much do you charge?" This may signal that the customer is focused on drilling down to the cheapest possible option versus making sure they are getting a quality product at a fair price.

Although designer Erin Fitzsimmons cringes when the conversation starts this way, she's learned to steer the focus to the project itself, tailoring her response to the individual:

> I've worked with both first time and self-publishing authors. Usually this means low budget, tight schedule, and lots of work outside the realm of "book design." I often get e-mails with a very vague description of a book project and then, "How much do you charge?" This is my absolute least favorite question.

My first response is always something along the lines of "Well, it really depends on the project. I need more details to give an accurate estimate." There's no way to determine how much work will be involved from one book project to the next, so I try to gauge my client.

Do they seem like the type of person who will react poorly to a high estimate? Or who will appreciate an exact number? Or perhaps they'd react well to a range? Every situation is different, but I always gather all the information first, then get back to them with my rate.

This is even more important as your business grows and you take on bigger projects. If you find that negotiation is not your strength and you continually quote too low (and thus don't get paid what you're worth) or quote too high (and potentially lose customers), maybe it's time to get some help.

Consider the process of business owner Maya:

Here is the most important thing my business partner and I have learned about quoting projects. Get all the information about the project *first*, before quoting any hourly or project rates. The way we do this is to have an initial kickoff meeting or phone call, gather all the details, then step away. We then follow up with a clearly written quote via e-mail the following day. Do *not* agree to anything in person, on the phone, or on the spot.

The best part is, we have a secret weapon! My husband is a director of compensation at a major company, and just a natural numbers guy. My business partner and I typically come up with a quote for the project, then have my husband verify our logic and our math as well as the language we use.

Not everyone has an in-house compensation expert like we do, but we all have a friend in our industry to bounce it off of, or a friend in another field who is great with numbers. Double-checking helps us negotiate with confidence, to the point where we now negotiate with Harvard MBAs and presidents of companies with relative ease. It's still stressful at times, but if you can logically talk to how you arrived at the quote, the conversation usually goes in a better direction.

5. Beware of working with friends, barter, and free advice

In any profession, there will be times when friends and family come to you for advice. As an expert in what you do, you might feel it can be flattering and rewarding to help others. As a natural-born techie, I don't mind when people come to me and want my opinion on what laptop or flatscreen TV to buy, and I'll even do some of the research for them if they want. I enjoy it.

In fact, sometimes it actually makes me angry when someone *doesn't* come to me first. Recently one of my best friends called me and said, "I just bought a new phone!" I half-jokingly reprimanded her, "What? You didn't consult me first?" She replied, "I was just tired of my BlackBerry freezing up on me and acting funny, so I stopped by a wireless store, asked what they had, traded my old one in, and walked out with a new Android phone fifteen minutes later."

When I heard that, I couldn't control my sarcasm. I politely said "Oh that's nice, Jayme. A phone's not really a big deal, and you can just change your mind later." She said, "Really?" I (laughingly) shouted back, "*No, not really!* Your phone is the single most important electronic device that you own! You use it sixteen hours a day, every single day of the entire year! You use it to check work e-mail, check personal e-mail, call people, text people, listen to music, and take photos! There are dozens and dozens of new Android phones coming out every single week, and while some are very, very good, others have horrible battery life, poor call quality, and received terrible reviews! And on top of that, you just signed a *legal contract* binding you to this decision for *two years*!"

After my mini-rant, she had the last word, shooting back at me, "Relax—I have thirty days to try it out." Why wasn't I surprised she had everything covered? Nothing scares her—she negotiates real estate deals in Manhattan.

So clearly, there are some cases when you are more than happy to help out a friend. But as a freelancer, what happens when a friend or family member comes to you and asks you to "help out" on a project?

Like anything else, you're going to have to weigh the options. Do you risk offending the person if you say no? Or do you take a hard line that this is your job—they wouldn't ask a doctor friend for a free physical, right?

Marina Fish said, "If people don't know exactly what you do or how much work is involved, they won't value it. I hate when someone says, 'This should only take you fifteen to twenty minutes, right?' So what I learned is that I will either just do something gratis or bow out completely. I don't bother trying to determine some kind of 'friends and family' rate or anything; it just gets too complicated."

And speaking of complicated scenarios, what about bartering goods or services for your work? While it sounds good in theory, it's very difficult to balance the amount of work evenly without one party feeling taken advantage of.

Fish told me, "Having a few negative experiences with bartering has made me basically stop considering it at all. If I did it again, I would have a much clearer contract, with expectations spelled out more clearly than I have in the past."

Fitzsimmons felt the same way, stating, "The most frustrating freelance project I was involved in was actually one where I agreed to barter with a jewelry designer in exchange for monetary fees. I was photographing their pieces for the website, and ended up doing hours and hours of retouching work that was not originally included in the budget.

"The tricky thing about barter is when you're not convinced that the goods being bartered for are worth the dollar amount promised. So for, let's say, eight hours of work, I was offered a $400 pair of cuff links. The problem with that is, I would never personally spend $400 on cuff links. So that was where we needed to renegotiate."

Often times, a prospective client will e-mail you a bunch of questions about their project, corner you at a cocktail party, or offer to buy you a cup of coffee in order to "pick your brain" on your field of expertise.

Sometimes the person is absolutely genuine and wants to learn more, or they may not even realize that they are asking for things that you usually charge for. But in some cases, individuals have a more dishonorable intent, purposely trying to solicit advice without having to pay for it, or using you as a source of information and pricing in order to have leverage against a company they are already working with.

While you'll need to keep your guard up and go with your gut instinct to determine a person's motive, Facebook consultant Helen Todd has come up with a pretty good solution that works for her:

If prospective clients aren't a good fit, have a smaller budget than my range of services, or just seem to be digging for free advice, I direct them to my company's blog at fbadz.com, where there's tons of free information and resources for do-it-yourselfers.

For the most commonly asked questions I get, I provide links to specific posts and to my YouTube videos that explain the task. Right now I have nearly seventy-five links in various categories, covering everything from "getting started" guides to our favorite third-party ad managers.

One of the most common questions I get is "How do I set up a custom Welcome Tab on Facebook?" So I created a four-minute YouTube video that walks you through the entire process. Now, instead of having to explain it hundreds of times, I just e-mail them the link.

The initial setup and production of these pages took a little bit of work, but it's been an enormous time-saver in the long run while also serving to establish my expertise in the field for those clients who are a good fit.

If all else fails, designer/illustrator/typographer Jessica Hische put together an amusing infographic for freelancers called Should I Work for Free? (http://shouldiworkforfree.com).

6. Keep projects within scope and prevent "feature creep"

Okay, so you've found a good client, you begin doing all the work you talked about in the kickoff meeting—but, slowly but surely, they keep adding on more and more tasks. It's not unlike deciding to repaint your kitchen. Once you see how that looks, suddenly your cabinets look outdated. Then when you replace those, it makes the appliances look old. And if you're going to update the fridge and the stove, then you might as well put down some new hardwood floors. The money and to-do list adds up in a hurry.

A well-respected freelancer will have the ability to remind the client of their original goals and gently steer them back on track. But if that doesn't work, there are a few other options.

One option is simply to bill your client hourly instead of on a per-project basis. I know many a web designer who can tell the tale of watching a redesign spiral out of control, as marketing, editorial, sales, and management all feel they need to put their input into a design.

It can be incredibly frustrating for the designer to watch as their previously streamlined design gets increasingly cluttered by new features, not to mention that it fits poorly in their portfolio. (Keep those original mockups handy!)

© iStockphoto.com/MarcusPhoto1

But if designers are powerless to control change after change, the redeeming quality of an hourly rate is that the longer the project goes on, the more it pays.

For freelancers being paid on a per-project basis, the key is to specify as much as possible in a written contract before starting work. Then, as new features are proposed, you have a working document to reflect back on and say that anything beyond that scope will require additional fees.

Andrew Hammer is a New York–based freelance photographer, and also a performing clown for Looney Lenny's Clown-o-rific (http://www.clownorific.com)—and you thought this book was going to be all business.

Regarding his photography business, Hammer stated:

> My biggest lesson was to make sure both sides are on the same page. I definitely got taken advantage of more than once because I didn't use contracts early on in my career—even just a one-page agreement would have been enough.
>
> Especially with photographic images, people tend to take advantage and know you will probably never see any of the various violations because it's too hard for me to continually search all forms of media to make sure they've credited me properly. But now I always have a standard contract I work with, including a clause dealing with the misuse and proper crediting of images, which helps me both in the short-term and if anything else comes up down the line.

7. Get paid in a timely manner

If you're a full-time employee, unless your company is under some financial strain, you can pretty much count on your paycheck hitting direct deposit every two weeks like clockwork. That is not always the case

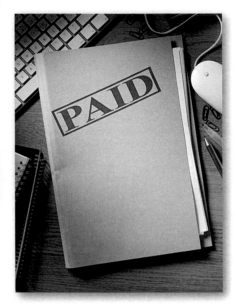

with freelancers. Because you are often dealing with individuals, the collection process can take longer than expected.

What are ways a freelancer can make sure they get their negotiated compensation on time?

The first thing you need to do is familiarize yourself with how some companies work, and what the terms of payment are.

Maya recalled the following:

> During our first year of business we did a project around Columbus Day in October and didn't get paid until January or February. The term "Net 30" meant nothing to me before we started our business, but now it's part of our daily language.

> If a payment is late, don't be afraid to play "collections." Call the person you did the work for and don't be afraid to follow up. Don't be shy. Be kind. Be firm. But do follow up when the check doesn't arrive when it is supposed to.

Hopefully over time your business can pick and choose customers and drop the ones that don't pay their bills. But what about a worst-case scenario? Marina Fish, the Seattle designer, said, "There were a small handful of times where payment was so late that I had to threaten to keep native files until my invoices were paid, but not very often."

One last approach is to have late fees written into the contract—a little incentive never hurts to get clients to pay on time.

8. Keep track of business details (even when you're the creative person)

When walking into a salary negotiation for a new job, the most important thing you can have is information. As they say, the devil is in the details.

In my life I've been fortunate to know many fantastic graphic designers and artists, and without fail I get along with them instantly. I believe that our personalities always mesh because we complement each other. I tend to be very analytical, dealing with facts and numbers, while designers have the unique ability to see the big picture and deal with colors and shapes.

However, the skills that give them their biggest strength generally leads to their largest weakness—the business side of things. Most of the designers I know just want to do one thing, and that is create.

Because keeping track of details can help their business in so many ways, there are two tactics that smart freelancers can employ: simplify or outsource.

Stacey Asato (http://www.asatodesign.com) was the lead designer in my group while at ESPN.com, and she now runs her own business in Seattle. She told me the following:

> To tell you the truth, I used to be terrible at keeping track of the business side of things. I'd get so absorbed with my love of design on a project, that I would lose track of the hours I spent on it. However, within the last couple of years I have started to use time tracking and it really helps monitor the number of hours that I work.
>
> This is especially helpful when I am working on multiple projects, since I can just jump back and forth between them and it keeps track of everything for me. Currently I am using a free time-tracking program called Toggl, and an invoicing program called Harvest.

While there are dozens of programs available, here is a short list of ones to check out:

Simple time tracking

- Toggl (http://www.toggl.com)
- The Invoice Machine (http://invoicemachine.com)

Full-featured time tracking, invoicing, and client management

- FreshBooks (http://www.freshbooks.com)
- Harvest (http://www.getharvest.com)
- Billings (http://www.marketcircle.com/billings)
- On The Job (http://stuntsoftware.com/onthejob)

The other way to handle billing is outsourcing. Even if you're just a one-person shop like Marina Fish Design, if it frees your time up to do what you do best, it will be money well spent:

This might be the single best thing I ever did for my business: I hired a bookkeeper/personal accountant. She makes sure my estimated taxes are on time, my licenses updated, my business expenses recorded, files everything from receipts to creative ideas/sketches, and a bunch of other things.

She's paid for herself numerous times, and allows me to do what I'm efficient at, instead of spending time doing things I'm less good at (like never-ending paperwork) and that I find easy to put off. She comes once a week, at a certain time. This keeps the hours low, because we can keep up on tasks. During this scheduled time I also do personal finances, make financial plans for the future, etc. It is so worth it.

While your first instinct might be to avoid paying for client management software or a bookkeeper, remember that "presentation is everything." Todd said, "If everything from my website to invoices looks professional, it instills confidence in my clients for my services and subtly reinforces the fee I'm charging them, too."

9. Increasing the rate that you charge your clients

As a freelancer, getting a raise is easy. Since you're the boss, just ask yourself if you want to make more money. The hard part, however, is passing on this new rate to your clients, especially existing ones. In order to do so, you're going to have to make a convincing argument.

Let's go back to the case of Helen Todd, the freelance social media consultant from Step 2, who took on a higher-end luxury client for a six-month contract at a reduced rate when her business was just getting off the ground.

But now that the six months are over, is she forced to renew them at the original rate? Here's a case where she truly put her negotiation skills to work:

During the original contract work, one critical step was to create monthly reports. This showed the company's progress in social media and my services that helped achieve the growth. By the time we were ready to talk about renewing the contract, both the client and I knew that my company should be getting paid more. Not only did we have a successful six months, but my company had also shown that it was credible and not going anywhere.

But the question lingered: How much more should I charge? That was a hard question. I wrote down in a very detailed list exactly all of the different services that I did for the client. Comparing that to the original contract, the list was quite extensive.

I also calculated the ballpark amount of time each different task took—even I was surprised at the total time that was being allocated every month. My concerns included overshooting the monthly fee or undervaluing and still not getting paid what I was worth. In the end, I aimed high and knew exactly the monthly fee range I was comfortable with.

So my strategy went like this:

- I made an extremely detailed list of every task my company helped the client with, which was categorized and had monthly hours attached to it.
- I then calculated my per hour rate against these hours to show the value of services that my company was providing.

Before meeting in person to discuss the new contract,

- I summarized the enormous success we had with the client to reinforce the value of our services.
- I determined the monthly fee I'd be comfortable with in order to do *all* of the services listed, so I could break out individual tasks if needed.

When I broke down the retainer fee I included:

- An estimated range of monthly hours
- My company's hourly rate
- Range of monthly retainer fee
- Total proposed monthly retainer fee (a figure in the middle of the range)

- Re-signing contract discount
- Six-month contract discount
- Total monthly retainer

When the big moment for negotiation came, the client mentioned that he was expecting a higher fee—but not that high.

I agreed with him and told him I was surprised myself, but putting it all on paper made both of us realize the amount of time that the monthly tasks truly demanded. What this did was let the math speak for itself and not appear that I was subjectively asking for a higher fee.

This allowed me to work from a position of strength, letting me say that we could either continue to do all of these tasks at the fee I proposed, or take some away so that I could continue to grow as a company.

The flexibility in the proposal said, "I can work within your budget depending on how you want to continue," and the client had the option to bring some of the tasks he was previously giving to my company in-house.

In the end, the client ended up presenting what he had in mind for a monthly budget and asked if we could continue like before, without keeping track of hours or cutting back on my services. For me, the fee was right within the range that I was thinking (remember I aimed high) and the proposal reinforced the value of the services the client was getting. It didn't hurt that they also wanted to sign a one-year contract, so I said yes, and it was a win-win situation.

In the previous scenario, Helen did an amazing job upselling her client after proving her worth. In fact, this is how countless businesses that are just starting out make their name and get off the ground.

What if you're just starting out but know that your skills are in very high demand? What if you have twenty years of working experience and *then* decide to start your own company? Do you still have to work from the ground up? One alternative that may seem counterintuitive is to flip this model on its head. In other words, you position your business by charging *much more* than the competition.

Psychologically, if you approach a freelancer and receive a quote that is well below what you expected, you may question the professionalism and quality of their service. You might be worried that they are not as good as an experienced freelancer. Conversely, if the quote is at the top of your range, it can set the expectation that you are getting the very best. Everyone has heard the phrase "You get what you pay for."

By using this angle, you can receive the maximum payment for your services and aim for a higher level of clientele. But beware—everything from your work to your correspondence to your level of support better be up to par, or that business won't keep coming back.

10. Experience is the best teacher

In conducting my interviews, one thing was clear: There's no substitute for experience. Every freelancer is different and conducts business in his or her own way, which is part of the excitement of working on your own.

You will make some mistakes and have some growing pains along the way, but if you can harness some of the negotiation techniques from earlier in the book and combine them with the advice in this chapter, you should come out ahead far more often than not.

Conclusion

At the beginning of this book, I asked you to think back on your childhood, and what you wanted to be when you grew up.

Perhaps your father was a doctor, and his father before him was a doctor, so there was never any doubt that you would follow in their footsteps.

There's also a good chance you will spend your career exploring a diverse number of jobs, relocating to and experiencing new places, learning from smart coworkers, and succeeding and failing along the way before eventually discovering what you were truly meant to do. If that's the journey you've taken, consider yourself fortunate.

And just maybe this book has served as a catalyst to give you the information and confidence necessary to make a real difference in your life, while entertaining you a little along the way. If that's the case, I'm thrilled because we've achieved our two goals.

1. Was I prepared?

You now know the secret negotiating techniques that no one ever taught you. Over time, some of the data, technology, and sources of information will change. I urge you to visit SalaryTutor.com, where I will provide helpful articles, videos, and applications to arm you with the latest resources. Information will always be king.

2. Did I do everything I could?

During the research for the book, I always asked people how their last negotiation went. More often than not, a look of disappointment immediately washed over their faces, and they told me they just accepted the original offer that was given them. When I asked why they didn't make a counteroffer, they often answered, "I didn't know I could!"

Sometimes all it takes is simply seeing someone else do it first. For example, it took more than one hundred years, from 1853 to 1954, for the world's greatest runners to improve their time in the mile from 4:28 to 4:01.3. But they still had not broken the magic 4-minute barrier. Many thought it was impossible. However, after Roger Bannister ran a 3:59.4 on May 6, 1954—proving it could be done—John Landy ran a 3:57.9 just 46 days later.

Now that you've seen real-world examples of how negotiations have been done, you should have the proper mind-set and confidence to accomplish it yourself.

In the end, of course, it's not just about the money. My hope is that someday you'll be able to look back on your career and say that you did what you set out to do, had fun doing it, and were compensated fairly along the way. Every day might not be a dream, and you might not win every negotiation, but if you do the right research and are prepared, you'll be able to say you did everything you could.

Thanks,

Jim Hopkinson

Acknowledgments

Special thanks to:

Erin Fitzsimmons | Book Designer

Erin is the incredibly talented designer of my original book layout, masterfully melding the 24,000-plus flowing words of my manuscript with the images and bullet points from my 347-page PowerPoint presentation—all without a complaint. She has worked as a photo editor, an art director, and a designer at companies such as *People* magazine, Fairchild Publications, and HarperCollins Children's division.

You can find her work at http://www.efitzdesign.com.

Brandon Werner | Web and Logo Designer

Brandon has been referred to as my "Intern 1.0" at Wired.com, so it's no surprise that he is an early adopter of all things tech himself. He designed both the original logo and website presence for SalaryTutor .com, as well as my personal blog and podcast, *The Hopkinson Report*. His skill set includes design, illustration, WordPress, video, podcasting, and anything else with the word *media* in it.

You can find his work at http://www.TheModernDayPirates.com.

Jean O'Halloran

Jean has worked as an editor at major publishers such as Little, Brown and also at a much more challenging occupation: high school English teacher. She has an English degree from Providence College, a master's in Language and Literacy from Harvard University (which means she's wicked smaht), and took the arduous first pass through my original manuscript. She lives in Massachusetts with her husband, Brian; sons Sean and Sam; daughter, Abby; and golden retriever, Roy. She's one of the coolest, friendliest, and nicest people I know, and I'm not just saying that because she's my sister. Like her older brother, she enjoys finding typos on restaurant menus.

Friends and Family

I'd like to thank my parents, Fred and Joanne; my brother, Paul; my agent, Jim Levine; the team at Business Plus including Leah Tracosas, Meredith Haggerty, Jen Musico, Liz Kessler, Tom Whatley, Dylan Hoke, and Rick Wolff; and all the other incredibly supportive friends and family members who have had to listen to me talk about this passion project for several years.

Please stay in touch and provide your feedback:

E-mail: Jim@SalaryTutor.com

Twitter: @SalaryTutor

Web: www.SalaryTutor.com

Check out the Business Plus blog at:

www.businessplusblog.com

Salary Tutor
www.salarytutor.com

Negotiation Cheatsheet

Before you start:

1. Target a job you are passionate about.

2. Determine the salary range using personal networking, online research, and social media.

3. Create an "IRS Document," Industry Research of Salaries.

4. Don't give salary history on an application. Write "To be discussed during interview" or "Negotiable."

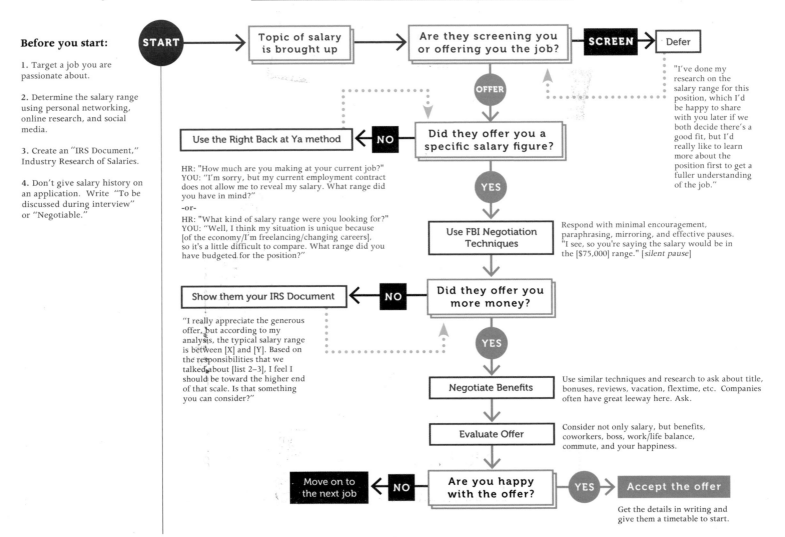

START → **Topic of salary is brought up** → **Are they screening you or offering you the job?** → **SCREEN** → Defer

"I've done my research on the salary range for this position, which I'd be happy to share with you later if we both decide there's a good fit, but I'd really like to learn more about the position first to get a fuller understanding of the job."

OFFER

Did they offer you a specific salary figure? — **NO** → **Use the Right Back at Ya method**

HR: "How much are you making at your current job?"
YOU: "I'm sorry, but my current employment contract does not allow me to reveal my salary. What range did you have in mind?"
-or-
HR: "What kind of salary range were you looking for?"
YOU: "Well, I think my situation is unique because [of the economy/I'm freelancing/changing careers], so it's a little difficult to compare. What range did you have budgeted for the position?"

YES

Use FBI Negotiation Techniques

Respond with minimal encouragement, paraphrasing, mirroring, and effective pauses. "I see, so you're saying the salary would be in the [$75,000] range." [*silent pause*]

Did they offer you more money? — **NO** → **Show them your IRS Document**

"I really appreciate the generous offer, but according to my analysis, the typical salary range is between [X] and [Y]. Based on the responsibilities that we talked about [list 2–3], I feel I should be toward the higher end of that scale. Is that something you can consider?"

YES

Negotiate Benefits

Use similar techniques and research to ask about title, bonuses, reviews, vacation, flextime, etc. Companies often have great leeway here. Ask.

Evaluate Offer

Consider not only salary, but benefits, coworkers, boss, work/life balance, commute, and your happiness.

Are you happy with the offer? — **NO** → **Move on to the next job**

YES → **Accept the offer**

Get the details in writing and give them a timetable to start.

Image: Robin Richards